HOME OFFICE

REPORT OF THE ENQUIRY INTO THE ESCAPE OF SIX PRISONERS FROM THE SPECIAL SECURITY UNIT AT WHITEMOOR PRISON, CAMBRIDGESHIRE, ON FRIDAY 9th SEPTEMBER 1994

By Sir John Woodcock, CBE, QPM.

*Presented to Parliament by the Secretary of State
for the Home Department
by Command of Her Majesty
December 1994*

LONDON: HMSO
£16.50 net

Cm 2741

The Rt Hon Michael Howard QC MP,
Secretary of State for The Home Department,
50, Queen Anne's Gate,
LONDON,
SW1H 9AT.

12th December 1994

Dear Home Secretary,

This is the report of the Enquiry into the escape of six prisoners from the Special Security Unit at Whitemoor Prison, Cambridgeshire, on Friday 9th September 1994.

I thank the Commissioners of the Metropolitan and City of London Police and the Chief Constables of Bedfordshire and Essex for making staff available to work in my Enquiry Team. I would also like to thank the Director General of the Prison Service for the secondment of one of his senior staff to act as liaison officer.

I now submit this report to you.

Yours Sincerely,

Sir John Woodcock, CBE, QPM.

Enquiry Team

Sir John Woodcock, CBE, QPM

Deputy Assistant Commissioner Alan Fry, QPM

Interview team -

Detective Chief Superintendent	Tom Glendinning	- Metropolitan
Detective Inspectors	Andrew Sellers	- Metropolitan
	Mike Barley	- Metropolitan
Detective Sergeants	Bernard Emslie	- City of London
	Philip Young	- City of London
	Kay Meiklejohn	- Essex
	David Marshall	- Metropolitan
Detective Constable	Jim Johnstone	- Metropolitan

Report compilation and research -

Superintendent	Peter Todd	- Bedfordshire
Detective Sergeant	Peter Thurlow	- Metropolitan
Detective Constable	Russ Dunlop	- Metropolitan

Secretariat -

Mrs Rachelle Hembury	- Home Office
Miss Angela Travers	- Home Office

Prison Service liaison -

Mr Peter Kitteridge	- Area Manager (London South)

Contents

Appendices

Section 1: Overview

(i) INTRODUCTION

1.1 It was 8.10p.m. on Friday, 9th September 1994, when the concentration of the prison officers in the Special Security Unit (SSU) at Whitemoor Prison was disrupted by a telephone call announcing that several of their charges were in the process of escaping over the prison wall. Until that time, 4 of the 7 officers on duty in the unit had been playing a game of Scrabble; a fifth was reading whilst the remaining two were busying themselves in the control room. All were no doubt looking forward to the impending end to their evening shift, at 8.45p.m. It had been, until then, a normal, quiet shift in the SSU.

1.2 As a new and relatively 'high tech' prison, opened in 1991, HMP Whitemoor, located just north of March in Cambridgeshire, was regarded within the service as virtually escape-proof. Unlike many of the older prisons, the highest levels of security had been incorporated in a 'green-field' situation, and the SSU was the most protected area of the whole site, situated behind no fewer than 2 walls and a fence; it was seen as a prison within a prison, with the label of "impregnable" often assigned to it.

1.3 On 9th September, the SSU housed 10 of the highest risk inmates in the prison system, all rating as Category A (exceptional risk); this rating signifies, in Prison Service terms, those inmates who are the very highest security risk and considered to "pose a danger to the public, the police or the security of the state". Despite the violent reputation of such inmates, however, work in the SSU was generally regarded by staff as unchallenging. Unlike other wings in Whitemoor, there were comparatively few problems with disruptive inmates, but the potential was always present. The regime allowed for a high degree of recreation and movement of prisoners internally, placing confidence in the high level of physical security surrounding the Unit. In fact, as one officer later described it, the Unit virtually ran itself and provided staff with a reasonably easy, if somewhat tedious, working day.

1.4 By 8.20 p.m. on this particular night, any delusion of impregnability had been totally and dramatically shattered as it became clear that 6 of the 10 SSU inmates had breached all the security measures. They had cut through the wire fencing of the exercise yard, scaled the inner wall, breached a further wire-mesh security fence and finally climbed over the outer wall. To assist the escape they had taken with them a vast array of largely self-manufactured equipment, including about thirty feet of rope ladder, made from plaited string with wooden rungs, poles to support the ladder and a metal clamping device adapted to fit exactly over the top of the inner wall, to support other ropes. They had ropes, made from torn mattress covers and string, bolt croppers, a torch and a number of smaller tools. More alarmingly, they also took with them two pistols, ammunition and a willingness to use them.

1

1.5 As rapidly descending darkness threatened to assist the inmates in their flight, prison staff and local police implemented a joint contingency plan which it had been hoped would only ever be of academic interest, or perhaps provide material for a table-top exercise. This was no exercise, however, the people escaping were 5 IRA terrorists and a man involved in a previous armed prison escape. The stakes in this game were the highest possible.

1.6 In fact, by a combination of effective contingency plans, good fortune and individual bravery, involving both prison staff and police officers, all 6 would-be escapees were recaptured within a short distance of the prison but not before one Prison Officer had been shot and 2 of the escapees had evaded searching officers for over 2 hours.

1.7 Fortune had played its part when the escapees chose the period of descending darkness, immediately before shift change-over, to make their move. The on-coming night shift were fortuitously placed, outside the walls, to augment their late shift colleagues who had to run from various parts of the prison and negotiate security systems, properly in place, before they were in a position to thwart the escapees.

1.8 Another essential element was the availability of the Essex Police helicopter, with thermal imaging capacity, which joined the search. Its deployment proved vital in locating the last two escapees.

1.9 Bravery was in evidence when, despite one officer already having been shot, and further rounds fired, unarmed prison staff and police officers maintained their pursuit and effected the recapture of the escapees.

1.10 After the euphoria of the recapture, the uncomfortable questions rapidly followed. The media, prison management, the Government and the public all demanded to know how such an outrage could have happened, and in particular at a flagship top-security prison.

1.11 The Woodcock Enquiry was formally announced on Saturday 10th September 1994, when the Home Secretary asked Sir John Woodcock, former HM Chief Inspector of Constabulary, to lead an Enquiry with the following terms of reference:-

> *"To enquire into all the circumstances surrounding the escape of*
> *six prisoners from the Special Secure Unit of Whitemoor Prison on the evening of*
> *Friday 9th September 1994, to report his conclusions to the*
> *Home Secretary and to make recommendations on any action that*
> *should be taken to avoid any recurrence."*

1.12 In parallel to this Enquiry, Cambridgeshire Constabulary established a criminal investigation into the escape and the shooting. It was during the course of their painstaking search of the vast array of personal property belonging to the SSU prisoners that subsequently (22nd September 1994), a further chapter of the drama unfolded when about one pound of Semtex explosive, short fuses and 3 detonators were discovered within the prison, concealed in the false bottom of an inmate's artists paint box.

1.13 The media, meanwhile, staged their own 'public' enquiry and delved ever more deeply into all aspects of the operation of Whitemoor Prison. They produced a host of allegations of bad practice, including apparent examples of lax security, ineffective searching routines, and an extraordinary catalogue of unearned privileges for SSU inmates. The latter included accounts of lavishly extravagant meals and inordinately high personal telephone bills, allegedly at the tax payer's expense.

1.14 At a juncture in history where the IRA ceasefire was in force and with movement towards some form of peace accord, the media also alleged a political motive to some or all of the additional privileges and the word "appeasement" became widely used.

(ii) METHODOLOGY OF THE ENQUIRY

1.15 The Enquiry Team consisted of police officers from Bedfordshire, the City of London, Essex and the Metropolitan police forces, based in London and at Whitemoor Prison. Secretarial support was provided by the Home Office and a senior liaison officer by the Prison Service.

(a) Information collection -

1.16 At the outset an open letter was circulated at Whitemoor and throughout the Prison Service setting out the 'terms of reference' of the Enquiry and inviting members of the Service to contact the Enquiry Team direct if they felt that they could in any way assist. This letter emphasised that the Enquiry had no disciplinary function and gave details of a PO box number for confidential responses.

1.17 Information was collated from personal interviews with :-

■ staff, presently and previously employed at Whitemoor,

■ Home Office Prison Service personnel,

■ other key individuals (e.g. Board of Visitors and Building Project Manager), and

■ other groups or individuals who asked to be interviewed.

1.18 Whitemoor Prison was visited extensively and Enquiry Team members spoke freely to staff and inmates. This resulted in the identification of a number of material witnesses who were subsequently formally interviewed. Over 100 officers were interviewed including virtually all the officers who had worked in the SSU and all those on duty at the time of the escape. Interviews were also undertaken with former Ministers of State, past and present Director Generals of the Prison Service, past and present Governors of the prison and all others with line command or policy formation responsibility. Some individuals were interviewed on a number of occasions and many of the interviews lasted a considerable number of hours.

1.19 Early contact was established with Cambridgeshire Constabulary, both at local and force level, with staff associations locally and nationally and with the Chief Inspector of Prisons. The 6 inmates involved in the escape were given the opportunity to be interviewed by the Enquiry Team but all declined.

1.20 The Team extracted information from a broad spectrum of documentary sources and from written submissions to the Enquiry from individuals, groups and on behalf of the Prison Service. Account was also taken of:

- Control Review Committee Working Party Report titled "Managing the Long-term Prison System" - 1984

- Home Office Research Study 109 on Special Security Units, published 1989

- Report by Rt Hon Lord Justice Woolf on Prison Disturbances April 1990

- Custody, Care and Justice: The Way Ahead for the Prison Service in England and Wales, 1991

- HM Chief Inspector of Prisons Inquiry into incident at HMP Brixton on 7 July 1991

- Lakes/Hadfield Report of an audit of the custody of Category A prisoners and an enquiry into DOC 1 Division - 1 November 1991

- HM Chief Inspector of Prisons Reports on HM Prison Whitemoor 1992 and 1994

- HM Prison Service Framework Document - April 1993

1.21 During the Enquiry a number of visits were paid to the following prison establishments:

Leicester

Belmarsh (South London)

Full Sutton (Nr York)

Parkhurst (Isle of Wight)

Frankland (Durham)

Maghaberry (Northern Ireland)

Maze (Northern Ireland)

These visits allowed a comparison of practice and procedure and provided further contextual detail to the Enquiry Team.

(b) Guiding principles of the Enquiry

Focus on the escape

1.22 The Enquiry Team quickly realised that the scale of the problems at Whitemoor was greater than simply the escape, and the finding of other unauthorised items in the possession of inmates was wholly predictable. However, a conscious decision was taken not to expand the terms of reference but to concentrate efforts towards answering the main questions connected directly to the actual escape. These questions are set out at the end of this section.

Target the truth

1.23 The aim of the Enquiry has always been to target the truth and not individuals. It was decided at an early stage that the final report of the Enquiry would be compiled in such a way as to avoid naming individuals and to reduce the temptation to seek scapegoats for errors and omissions which led to the escape. All assertions within the report are supported by substantial evidence.

1.24 A comprehensive and cohesive account emerged from the substantial number of interviews undertaken with a considerable amount of corroboration supported by documentary, video and forensic evidence. Inevitably there will be people who have information who have not been interviewed, not least the prisoners subject of the escape, but the Enquiry Team are totally satisfied that the truth has been established.

1.25 This report, as a whole, seeks to provide as complete an account of the issues surrounding the escape attempt as is possible, given the constraints of time, lack of co-operation of the inmates involved in the escape and the need to avoid compromising the criminal enquiry. It was essential to ensure that police primacy was maintained with no breach of sub judice rules. It must be accepted that other matters may still emerge, through the continuing criminal enquiry.

Confidentiality

1.26 From the outset all information provided to the Enquiry has been treated with total confidentiality. The early circulation stressed that the Enquiry had no disciplinary function and information provided would not be used in any proceedings without the consent of the contributor or by order of a court. Subsequent opportunities were taken to reinforce this message. Throughout the Enquiry there has been a high degree of co-operation and honesty from those interviewed.

Fairness

1.27 Every effort has been made to ensure fairness to those who have contributed to the Enquiry and anyone who might feel personally criticised in the final report.

1.28 Throughout the information gathering stage, every opportunity was taken to test provisional findings, criticisms and likely recommendations with individuals at all levels of the Prison Service.

1.29 As previously stated, no individuals are named in the final report. However, criticisms are made of practices and procedures that frequently relate to specific posts, which could lead to the identification of these postholders, at least within the Service. Once a draft report was completed, in keeping with best practice emanating from the Royal Commission on Tribunals of Inquiry (1966), under the chairmanship of Rt. Hon. Lord Justice Salmon, prior notification of the provisional findings of the Enquiry was circulated to 79 people who it was felt might believe they could be identified as subject of criticism within the report. The circulation offered an opportunity for individuals to challenge factual accuracy and identify any unfair criticism before the report was finalised.

1.30 Of those in receipt of "Salmon letters", responses were received from 22 persons, only 2 of whom were officers below Governor Grade, both of whom were very supportive of the emerging findings of the Enquiry. The Prison Governors Association responded on behalf of 6 recipients.

1.31 Every effort was made to accommodate recipients of Salmon letters. In doing so the submission deadline was extended and all requests for further individual interviews were met. A request for a joint meeting with 6 respondents was declined, in keeping with the underlying principle of individual confidentiality but each individual was offered the opportunity for further interview; one accepted and a lengthy and very positive meeting took place. All responses were carefully considered and, where necessary, suitable amendments or additions made to the Report.

1.32 Some of the replies emphasised disappointment that the Enquiry had not extended the Terms of Reference to include national problems and had dealt with the escape from the SSU in isolation of other issues which, in their view, impacted on events at Whitemoor. Concerns were raised regarding the many changes undertaken in the Service, the rising population, the need to strike a balance between care and control and the management difficulties of handling groupings of prisoners imposed upon Establishments. All these issues were seen as producing extra work and distractions, absorbing significant amounts of management time. Conversely, it was suggested the Enquiry had gone beyond the Terms of Reference which is an indication of the difficulties experienced of dealing with one incident without taking account of wider issues. Throughout, the Enquiry has remained steadfast in retaining a focus on the following 5 questions which are the basis of the main body of the Report.

(1) How did the inmates manufacture the escape equipment without being detected?

(2) How were so many articles stored and hidden from prison officers?

(3) How did the inmates obtain the firearms and explosives inside a high security prison?

(4) How did the escapees breach the security measures and reach the outer fence before the alarm was raised?

(5) Were there other factors in the regime of the SSU which assisted the escape?

1.33 The issues surrounding these main questions appear in Sections 4 - 8 of this report. Before these issues can be discussed in depth, however, it is necessary to understand the context within which the events of 9th September took place. Section 2 provides this background information, and Section 3 outlines the basic elements of the actual escape as the Enquiry Team believe it happened.

Section 2: Background Information

A. SOME TERMS EXPLAINED

2.1   Before explaining the events of 9th September, and looking more closely at the operation of the Special Security Unit at HMP Whitemoor, there are a number of terms used within the Prison Service which require definition for the benefit of the lay reader.

(i)   Dispersal prison

2.2   In the early 1960s there were no specially secure prisons in England and Wales. This lack of provision was clearly brought into focus by the escapes of two of the Great Train Robbers, Charles Wilson and Ronald Biggs (respectively from Birmingham in 1964 and Wandsworth in 1965) and the spy George Blake (from Wormwood Scrubs in 1966).

2.3   The first attempt to deal with this problem was the establishment, in 1965, of small Special Security Wings at Durham and Leicester, but these could not provide a permanent solution, due to the expense of setting them up and their oppressive conditions brought about by the fact that they were not purpose built. In 1966 Lord Mountbatten carried out an enquiry into Prison Service security and made a number of recommendations, including those set out below:-

(1)   prisoners should be divided into 4 categories, according to the degree of security necessary for their containment (A,B,C and D, with A the highest),

(2)   a policy of concentration of Category A prisoners should be adopted, utilising a purpose-built fortress prison on the Isle of Wight,

(3)   standards of security in other prisons should receive attention, and

(4)   in parallel to the increased security, physical surroundings should be improved and a liberal and constructive regime adopted in order to reduce tensions and the desire to escape.

2.4   Whilst the broad recommendations were accepted by the then Home Secretary, he asked the Advisory Council on the Penal System to consider the nature of the regime under which the long-term prisoners might be held. The Council appointed a sub-committee, under Professor Radzinowicz, which subsequently, in 1968, produced its report entitled, "The Regime for Long-term Prisoners in conditions of Maximum Security".

2.5   This report came out strongly against the "concentration" philosophy recommended by Mountbatten, and instead recommended a system of "dispersal", under which Category A prisoners would be dispersed among the larger prison population of three or four specially selected establishments, with appropriately up-graded perimeter security. In 1968, 7 prisons were selected and plans were put in hand for one further new establishment to be a dispersal prison.

(ii) Special Security Unit (SSU)

2.6 SSUs evolved from the same events that eventually produced the dispersal system, namely the escapes of 1964/5. It was quickly recognised, after Wilson's escape, that there was a need for highly secure units to house the very small number of prisoners who posed the greatest threat to the public. By August 1965 two Special Security Wings, at Durham and Leicester, had been established and started receiving appropriate prisoners, including the remaining 4 Great Train Robbers. Plans were also put in place to open a third such wing at Parkhurst, on the Isle of Wight.

2.7 Special Security Wings were expensive to establish and provided a very restricted and oppressive regime. Following the findings of Mountbatten and Radzinowicz, they became regarded as a temporary measure, pending the full introduction of the dispersal system, and the accompanying increased security at those establishments.

2.8 By 1978, with the emergence of the terrorist prisoners, and a number of others who would previously have been subject to the death penalty, it was increasingly recognised that there was a continuing demand for these small maximum security units. It was further recognised that the overall capacity needed to be increased and that such units should be purpose built, rather than being adapted wings in existing premises.

2.9 In 1988 the first purpose-built SSU was opened at Full Sutton near York; by that time the two existing units, at Leicester and Parkhurst, were desperately in need of attention. Leicester SSU had been recognised as unsuitable, due to cramped conditions and location within a non-dispersal ("local") prison. Parkhurst was in need of upgrading and refurbishment.

2.10 In mid-1989, having regard to the increasing demand, and a further high profile escape (by helicopter from Gartree Prison, Leicester), the decision was taken to build a second SSU within the confines of the next dispersal prison to be built. That transpired to be HMP Whitemoor.

B. WHITEMOOR PRISON

2.11 The prison occupies a 90 acre site covering part of the former railway marshalling yard at March in Cambridgeshire. Construction started in February 1988 and the first prisoners were received on 30th September 1991. Set in flat, open fenland, the prison is located about 2 miles north of March, just off the March to Wisbech road.

2.12 The main prison is surrounded by a high weld-mesh fence and, beyond that, by a wall with an anti-escape "beak" (a smooth, mainly tubular construction along the full length of the wall, with an angular protrusion on the inner face, providing a difficult overhang for climbers to negotiate).

2.13 Whitemoor was originally designed and intended as a Category B Training prison (i.e. to house Category B convicted inmates) but a decision was taken before construction was completed to upgrade physical security to allow it to operate as a dispersal prison and to include a purpose-built SSU. The prison acts as a national resource for life sentence, vulnerable and Category A prisoners.

2.14 The decisions to change the designation of the prison at Whitemoor, and then to add an SSU, were taken almost independently of each other. The need for additional dispersal accommodation was wholly accepted and the upgrade was rapidly agreed. The addition of an SSU took somewhat longer, with debate over both the location and cost.

2.15 Although the change in designation of the main prison was understandable, it did have some adverse consequences. For example, no account had been taken of the higher staffing level required for a dispersal prison and there was, as a result, inadequate office space. There had also been no provision made for the greater amount of personal property acquired by dispersal prisoners. As a consequence, general storage space was insufficient and portable buildings had to be used from the outset. This situation was later eased by additional building provision.

2.16 There were also logistical problems encountered in identifying, selecting and co-ordinating the arrival of both staff and prisoners. The subsequent high proportion of vulnerable inmates also meant that the original design concept of free association could not be followed, resulting in much staff time and energy being devoted to maintaining segregation.

C. WHITEMOOR SSU

(i) Background

2.17 The need for a new SSU had been highlighted both by the Gartree Prison escape and by the worsening state of the existing units; the latter was described in official correspondence by the Home Office P3 Division:-

> *" There is continuing serious concern about the condition of the SSU building at Parkhurst, and to a lesser extent the Leicester Unit is far from satisfactory for its present role. Although the weaknesses and needs of both Units are being attended to, the solutions can only be short term."*

2.18 The basic construction of Whitemoor SSU was completed in September 1991 with an intention to receive prisoners in June 1992. Budget and staff were therefore arranged for the financial year commencing April 1992. The

Brixton escape resulted in a change of plan and it was decided to use the Whitemoor SSU to house Leicester SSU inmates from January 1992, for 3 months, whilst refurbishment took place at Leicester. The Unit was to be known as the "Leicester SSU at Whitemoor", and was staffed by a mixture of Leicester and Whitemoor officers.

2.19 The Unit remained open until February 1993, when it was closed to allow some structural alterations. It reopened in June 1993.

(ii) Premises

2.20 The SSU is located within the main prison boundaries, inside a second, uncapped concrete security wall; all walls and fences are in excess of 5 metres high.

2.21 At the time of the escape, the Whitemoor SSU consisted of one off-set cruciform shaped building with an adjoining exercise yard, totally enclosed by a single layer of weld-mesh fencing. The building housed 14 basic cells plus a small segregation area containing a further 3 cells. There were shower facilities, kitchen, TV room, hobbies room, studies area and gymnasium. The remainder of the building housed staff offices, control room, the inmate visits area and sundry plant and store rooms.

2.22 At the centre of the building was the general association area which abutted the exercise yard, the gym, the hobbies room and TV room. The general association area contained a pool table, a table and chairs and sundry board games and equipment for similar pursuits.

2.23 The Unit was equipped with closed circuit television (CCTV) cameras to the exterior, within the exercise yard, central association area, visits area and corridors. These cameras were monitored from the control room which, although it formed part of the building, was totally isolated from the prisoner areas and had a dedicated entrance. Other staff offices provided observation and access into the main communal areas.

(iii) Management structure

2.24 The management structure of the prison, as it was on 9th September, is set out in the chart, attached as Appendix 'A' to this report.

2.25 The SSU was a prison within a prison and as such was managed largely independently of the other wings. There was, however, a line management responsibility for the Unit through the main management structure, falling under the "Operations" grouping.

2.26 The SSU normally had a minimum of one Senior Officer (the first level of supervision) and six officers on duty at any time, drawn from a total SSU establishment of 26 officers. The duty staff would be deployed with two in the dedicated control room and the supervisor and four officers in the main prisoner areas of the Unit. A more detailed explanation of staffing roles, deployments and daily routines appears as Appendix 'B' to this report.

Section 3: The events of Friday 9th September 1994

3.1   Until 8.10 p.m., Friday 9th September had been a very normal shift within Whitemoor SSU. The full complement of 7 staff were on duty. The two officers allocated to the control room were monitoring an outgoing telephone call and the security cameras, respectively. The Senior Officer and three of those on General Duties were playing a game of scrabble and the fourth officer was reading a book; all five were located in the general association area of the Unit.

3.2   In the preparatory period and early stages of the escape, the majority of the self-made escape equipment, consisting of a wooden-runged rope ladder, other lengths of rope, metal poles and a clamping device, was probably passed out via the windows of the hobbies room, into the area called the sterile area which is located between the SSU building and the SSU security wall. This area was devoid of CCTV camera coverage.

3.3   The six escapees had each donned suitable clothing, with three of them wearing double sets of clothes thought to be in anticipation of a night on the Fens. They moved into the exercise yard, passing through the general association area unchallenged by staff. It was not the practice in the SSU for staff to supervise inmates in the exercise yard. Concealed within the escapees' possession were a pair of bolt croppers, a screwdriver, a stanley knife and a pair of pliers. They cut a hole in the exercise yard fence, which was not alarmed, bent back the cut area allowing entry into the sterile area and access to the SSU security wall.

3.4   They collected the rest of the escape equipment and, using the metal poles to provide support, the metal clamp, with a rope attached, was pushed up the face of the wall and lodged astride the top. The escapees then climbed the rope in turn, some descending the other side unobserved by SSU staff.

3.5   Whilst the tail-enders were still negotiating the first wall, the other escapees cut a section out of the next fence and forcefully bent back the resultant flap to gain access to the sterile area which is inside the outer wall. This action set off the fence alarm which alerted the Emergency Control Room (ECR) in the main prison.

3.6   Control staff watched incredulously as the CCTV screens revealed escaping inmates methodically climbing the outer wall, apparently unhurried by fear of challenge or recapture.

3.7   The ECR staff telephoned the SSU and alerted them of the escape in progress, by which time there was already an escapee at the outer wall. It was all happening in slow motion but everyone seemed powerless to stop it.

3.8   Jolted into action by the emergency telephone call, several SSU officers ran out into the exercise yard and one dived through the hole in the fence, into the sterile area. Although most of the escapees and equipment were by that time over the SSU wall, the officer saw the last two still climbing a rope and another one sitting astride the wall. He ran towards the rope, intending to tackle the last two inmates when he was hit by a bullet fired by the escapee sitting on top of the wall. Other officers assisted their injured colleague back into the exercise yard but this did not deter a number of other officers who had arrived from the segregation unit from entering the sterile area, under threat of being fired upon.

3.9   The other escapees had, meanwhile, passed through the second fence and set up the rope ladder at the outer prison wall to give access onto the beak. The ladder was attached to the top of the two sets of volleyball and badminton poles, adapted to fix end to end, and was supported by at least one guy rope. They put a further rope down the outside of the outer wall. This last rope was attached to the second fence, utilising a 'U' bolt clamp, and the end dropped over the top of the wall, to the ground below.

3.10   Whilst the ladder was being set up at the outer wall, one of the last escapees stood guard at the hole in the second fence, brandishing a pistol. Prison officers and a dog handler arrived at the area of the breach in the second fence; the gunman challenged them and fired at least one shot.

3.11   As the response progressed, staff were deployed both from within the prison and from the shift arriving for the start of their duty. At one stage there were four of the escapees perched on the top of the outer wall. As one of the escapees descended the outer wall, a dog handler approached him but was threatened with a pistol and backed away without releasing his dog. A group of officers gathered at the corner of the outer wall, outside the prison boundary and about 15 metres south of the escapees location.

3.12   Further officers stood near the inner fence, held at bay until the last man climbed the ladder. As the last escapee descended from the wall, however, a prison officer inside the establishment released the anchor point of the rope and the escapee fell heavily to the ground.

3.13   With all escapees down from the wall, they turned and ran northwards along the perimeter road, pursued at a short distance by the group of prison officers, including a number of dog handlers with dogs, some of which had been released from their leads. During the early stages of the pursuit one escapee fired one shot and then attempted to fire again at the officers but the gun appeared to jam. A substance, believed pepper, was thrown at the dogs.

3.14   Within a short distance of the prison, one escapee became isolated from the rest and was arrested by pursuing officers. The remaining five ran off towards the nearby nature trail, along the route of a disused railway line. About three-quarters of a mile along the trail the fleeing inmates were

Method of Escape

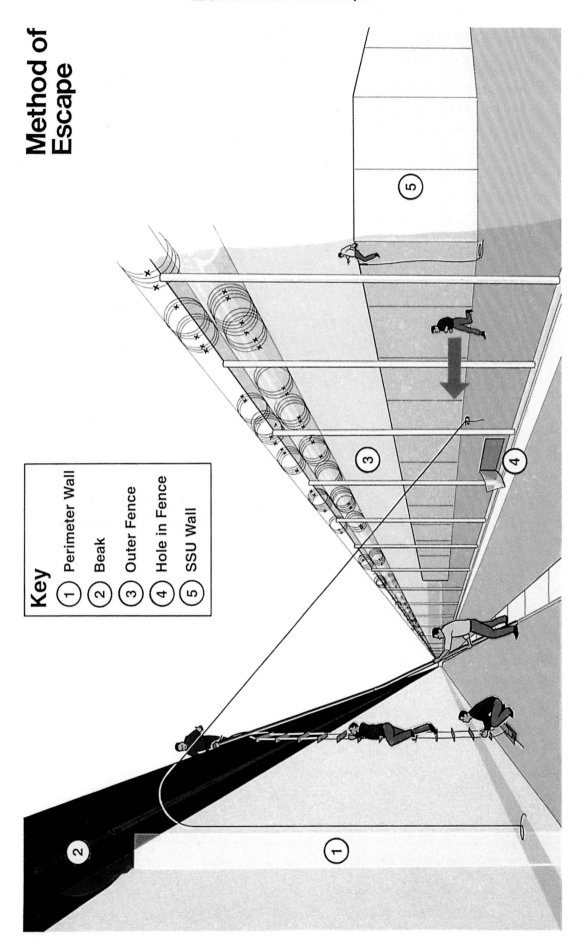

Key

1 Perimeter Wall
2 Beak
3 Outer Fence
4 Hole in Fence
5 SSU Wall

challenged by unarmed police officers with high powered torches, located on a railway bridge. Three of the escapees responded to a shouted instruction from the pursuing prison staff to lay down, perhaps believing the police to be armed.

3.15 The remaining two escapees branched off across surrounding fenland and went to ground. They were located some ninety minutes later by the use of a thermal imager operated from a police helicopter. They had hidden in vegetation at the base of a bank near the edge of a field, only a few feet from a main road. Officers on the ground were then directed to their location and the recapture was completed.

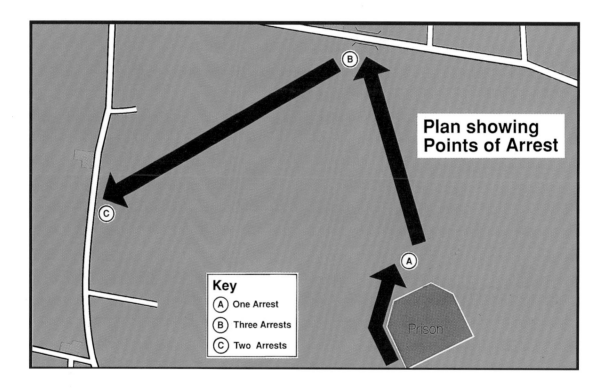

Plan showing
Points of Arrest

Key
(A) One Arrest
(B) Three Arrests
(C) Two Arrests

Prison

The Main Issues to be Addressed

As outlined in the Overview earlier, the Enquiry Team has concentrated its efforts on finding answers to 5 central questions, namely:-

■ How did the inmates manufacture the escape equipment without being detected?

■ How were so many articles stored and hidden from prison officers?

■ How did the inmates obtain the firearms and explosives inside a high security prison?

■ How did the escapees breach the security measures and reach the outer fence before the alarm was raised?

■ Were there other factors in the regime of the SSU which assisted the escape?

These questions are addressed by relating the events of 9th September and then considering the official instructions and procedures against the reality of practice as the Enquiry Team discovered it.

Section 4: How did the Inmates manufacture the escape equipment without being detected?

(I) EQUIPMENT USED IN THE ESCAPE

4.1   The essential equipment required to effect an escape from any tower or prison is, traditionally, a rope ladder made of knotted bedsheets. The Whitemoor escapees went several steps beyond such elementary materials. Of the vast array of items used in the escape, only a very limited number are considered to have been 'imported'; the majority had been manufactured, or adapted, on site.

4.2   The escapees had adapted the two sets of metal poles, intended to support badminton and volleyball nets, to enable them to be joined together end to end. Fixings from the weight training bar had been used to attach rope to the poles. They plaited string together to form something in excess of 200 feet of rope; some of which was then threaded through the seventeen identical wooden rungs, fashioned from 'scrap' wood, to make the ladder. Additional rope was made from string and bed mattresses, torn into strips, and plaited together. The items used are depicted in the sketch overpage.

4.3   The sketch depicts a pair of metal bolt croppers, constructed from a number of smaller parts. The cutting blades of this item were almost certainly smuggled into the SSU. A spanner was used to bolt the various elements together. The clamp used to bridge the inner wall was part of a television stand, dismantled some time earlier by the inmates. Other clamps, used to secure ropes, were apparently parts taken from inmates beds.

4.4   The escapees also took with them a total of £474.20 in cash, an improvised torch, made from a plastic box, a battery and various electrical parts. Searches subsequent to the escape also revealed that parts of a vacuum cleaner and a lawn mower had been removed, and hidden within the Unit, presumably for future use. Further unused pre-drilled lengths of wood, similar to those used as rungs in the ladder, and a box containing torn strips of mattress were found in the hobbies room.

4.5   When viewing the sketch and reading the list of equipment, it is impossible not to express concern that so many raw materials could have been gathered together and so much equipment made, presumably over a period of time, inside a Special Security Unit unnoticed by staff.

Items used or taken by Escapers

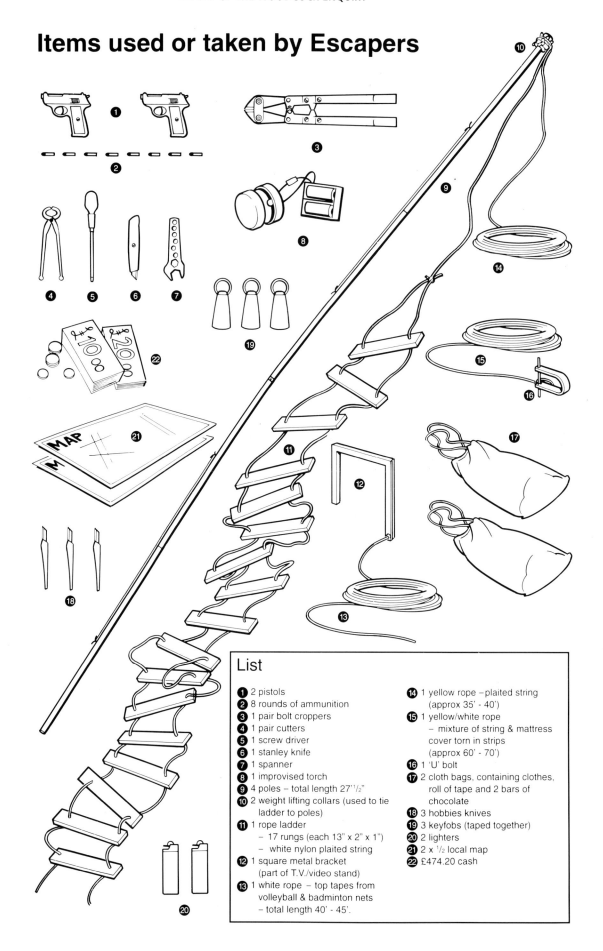

List

1. 2 pistols
2. 8 rounds of ammunition
3. 1 pair bolt croppers
4. 1 pair cutters
5. 1 screw driver
6. 1 stanley knife
7. 1 spanner
8. 1 improvised torch
9. 4 poles – total length 27'1/2"
10. 2 weight lifting collars (used to tie ladder to poles)
11. 1 rope ladder
    – 17 rungs (each 13" x 2" x 1")
    – white nylon plaited string
12. 1 square metal bracket (part of T.V./video stand)
13. 1 white rope – top tapes from volleyball & badminton nets – total length 40' - 45'.
14. 1 yellow rope – plaited string (approx 35' - 40')
15. 1 yellow/white rope – mixture of string & mattress cover torn in strips (approx 60' - 70')
16. 1 'U' bolt
17. 2 cloth bags, containing clothes, roll of tape and 2 bars of chocolate
18. 3 hobbies knives
19. 3 keyfobs (taped together)
20. 2 lighters
21. 2 x 1/2 local map
22. £474.20 cash

(II) SSU - FACILITIES TO MANUFACTURE

4.6 To understand the answer to this question, it is necessary to appreciate the layout within the unit and the ways in which facilities, provided for recreation and constructive activities, lent themselves perfectly to aid the manufacture of such equipment. The most relevant facilities to this aspect of the escape were the gymnasium, the TV room and, in particular, the hobbies room. There were no CCTV cameras in any of the communal rooms.

4.7 The gymnasium was equipped with several forms of exercise machines and there were also bars with loose weights, intended for use under supervision of a physical training instructor. Some equipment was put away in a store at the rear but the majority was left assembled or leaning against the walls in the main gym area. There was a window allowing prison officers in their main office to view into the room, and the door was located next to the office allowing easy access.

4.8 The TV room had a television, video recorder and several chairs. The room had three internal windows and a door from the general association area, to allow observation and monitoring by prison officers.

4.9 The hobbies room was located between the gym and TV room and was equipped with an assortment of wood, art equipment, including easels and canvasses, a sewing machine, a table-tennis table, two musical keyboards, a bench and a vice. At the rear of the main room there was a small storeroom, housing various overspill items from this and other rooms, including the badminton/volleyball supports and poles and a number of basic tools, attached to a "shadow board" (which had drawn outlines of all tools, for ease of checking).

4.10 In effect "hobbies room" was somewhat of a misnomer; with the level of equipment available it might more fittingly have been designated a workshop. The hobbies room/workshop had a large internal window, measuring over nine feet wide, providing visibility for the prison officers from the general association area.

4.11 Officers deployed within the main unit (4 officers on General Duties) were expected to be familiar with all prisoners in the SSU and to be aware of their location at all times whilst on duty. They also had a responsibility for checking the contents of the shadow boards and searching the communal areas after lock-up.

(III) THE PROCEDURES IN PRACTICE

4.12 With 4 officers responsible for maintaining a watch on the inmates, how did the manufacture of equipment take place unnoticed? The answer rests in the differences which existed between the procedures expected and those actually implemented.

(a) observation

4.13 The view into the TV room was wholly obscured by the fitting of

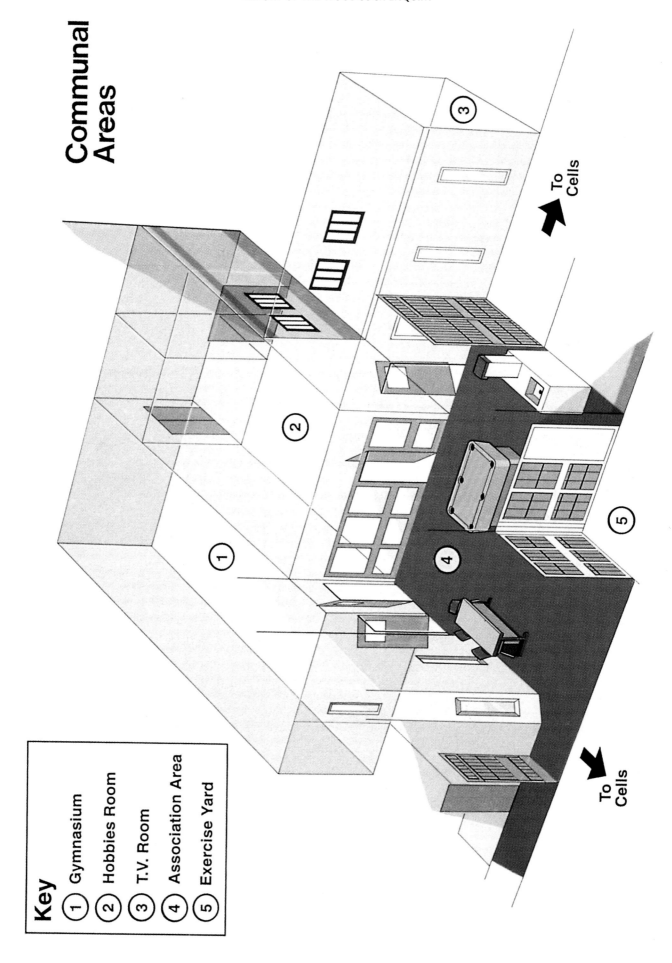

Communal Areas

Key

1. Gymnasium
2. Hobbies Room
3. T.V. Room
4. Association Area
5. Exercise Yard

To Cells

To Cells

venetian blinds to all of the internal windows. It is difficult to find their history but they were obviously erected officially, due to their permanence and fixings. The effect of the addition of these blinds was to render the room a visibility black-spot, limiting monitoring to staff intrusion into the room.

4.14   Observation from the staff office into the gymnasium, whilst not obscured by any blinds, could only be achieved through an act of virtual contortion due to the strategic siting of a refrigerator within the office, and the location of a large clock in the gym. The other views from the office were also restricted by both the size of the windows and their positioning.

4.15   With regard to the hobbies room, in January 1993 an inmate made long and loud protestations over the lack of privacy and demanded a curtain be fitted. He actually erected a bedsheet, which survived in situ for a few weeks. In February 1993 the Unit closed for refurbishment, opening again in June. The sheet was removed in the period of closure but returned soon after re-opening. By September 1993 the sheet had been replaced by net curtains, with two curtains having been provided by an officer, apparently as the best compromise achievable by the staff.

4.16   Having engineered the acquisition of two net curtains, one intended for change whilst the other was washed, the inmates duly erected both simultaneously leaving only the most shadowy of images available to any officer attempting to monitor activity, a fact verified by the Principal Officer. At the time of the escape any possible visibility had been further obscured by the positioning of a vertically folded table-tennis table and strategic location of an ever-increasing number of easels and canvasses.

4.17   The presence of the curtains reduced Officers' ability to supervise and caused the representatives of the Board of Visitors, an independent, statutory voluntary body consisting of local people appointed by the Secretary of State, to make repeated representation to the Governor to have them removed. This was of such concern that the Board raised it at their official meetings with the Governor on 4 separate occasions between February 1993 and February 1994.

4.18   In December 1993 the Governor had reported back to the Board that the

"..SSU staff were happy with them.."

and in February 1994 informed the Board of Visitors

*"..he did not feel that curtains in the SSU
represented a security risk.."*

It became clear from our interviews with staff that some were far from content while others were unconcerned about the curtains, nevertheless the result was that the prisoners got what they wanted.

4.19   It was not just the members of the Board and regular prison staff who were unhappy with the reduced visibility. On the morning of the escape, the part-time music teacher felt quite nervous in the hobbies room, with art canvasses and the table tennis table obscuring the staff view into the room. The potential for assault or a hostage situation was apparent. If so obvious to an outsider, it begs the question why the Governor did not recognise the implications of the reduced visibility.

(b)   patrolling and personal visits

4.20   Despite the drastically reduced visibility, with regular and extensive patrolling and visits into the communal areas it is difficult to understand how manufacture could have taken place. Unfortunately visits and patrolling were neither regular nor extensive. As one officer put it,

> *"..prisoners had no expectation of staff entering cells unannounced, because it rarely happened."*

Other officers summed up the predominant ethos within the Unit as having been, "don't upset the inmates and don't rock the boat."

4.21   It is also clear from interviews and observation that inmates generally could be very adept at distracting staff either by creating a false sense of security or even through stage-managed diversions.

(c)   audit of materials

4.22   The provision of materials for woodworking activities within the workshop was uncontrolled and included damaged prison property from the main prison. Additional materials had also been provided by well-intentioned staff members.

4.23   No audit was ever carried out on this store of materials nor any consideration given to the alternative uses to which it might be put. The ladder alone accounted for seventeen pieces of wood, each about a foot long, all of which had to be shaped and pre-drilled before being threaded onto the ropes.

4.24   The use of prison furniture was not a new phenomenon. As recently as November 1993 some inmates at Full Sutton Prison were found to have constructed the component parts of a ladder from pieces of wood like those used at Whitemoor. These inmates had also plaited together twine and torn bedcovers to form ropes.

4.25   At the meeting of the Category A Operations Group, held on 31st January 1994, this matter was discussed and it was agreed that pictures of the construction would be sent to dispersal Governors to enable them to alert staff. This was undertaken by staff at Full Sutton in March 1994.

4.26   Notification of the equipment manufacture was also circulated to all prisons in February 1994 by way of the Monthly Security Briefing although the item was very general, simply stating

> *"HMP Full Sutton found sophisticated escape equipment in the form of a ladder made from cell furniture. There has been evidence of such plans at other dispersals as well."*

(iv) Conclusions

4.27 For understandable reasons the inmates were provided with the tools and the materials for constructive hobby activities. It needed little imagination to realise that without the closest of supervision and observation such facilities and tools could become the instruments of escape. In such confinement, it was right and proper to provide worthwhile activities for inmates, but it was an indictment on Whitemoor that materials similar to those used in the Full Sutton escape attempt were allowed in abundance and unaudited, to be freely available in the SSU.

4.28 The reduced ability of staff to monitor visually activities in the communal room, and in particular in the workshop, was nothing short of scandalous. This had been contributed to by the apparent reluctance to upset the inmates by refusing their requests, however unreasonable.

RECOMMENDATIONS - (SURVEILLANCE AND OBSERVATION)

1.   CCTV should be extended to give coverage of all internal and external areas of the Unit, including the staff office but excluding personal cells and showers.

2.   All curtains, blinds and obstructions should be removed from internal observation windows throughout the Unit. The size and location of windows in the staff office should be reviewed as the present arrangement does not afford a view into one of the cell corridors. Consideration should be given to incorporating one-way glass to increase unobtrusive surveillance.

3.   Officers should patrol all areas of the Unit throughout their shift, entering all communal areas unannounced and at frequent but irregular intervals. The tasks allocated should rotate at least hourly, to guard against boredom and retain alertness.

4.   All materials, tools and equipment in communal/association rooms should be subject of daily formal audit. Consideration should be given to implementing good practice as at Full Sutton who have a tally system for knives and kitchen utensils. This could usefully be extended to include all tools and other potentially dangerous items. All items should be retained in, and allocated from, the staff office.

5.   Night duty staff to make regular, thorough and documented searches of all communal areas on a nightly basis, for unauthorised or suspicious items, as part of a certified searching pattern.

Section 5: How were so many articles stored and hidden from Prison Officers?

(I) STORAGE IMPLICATIONS FOR THE ESCAPE MATERIALS

5.1 As described previously, the array of equipment gathered together by the escapees was extensive and bulky; even in its most compacted form, it would have filled two wheelbarrows. In such a small Unit, it seems inconceivable that so much property, presumably pieced together over a period of time, could remain undiscovered.

5.2 Since the escape, there has been a thorough search of the whole Unit and the property kept elsewhere in storage. In addition to the escape equipment, the following items have been found:-

Item	Location found
Semtex Fuses Detonators	False bottom of artists paint box in storage
Hacksaw blade £10 in cash	Inside a transistor radio
6" ruler Knife Razor blade Bar of soap 4 metal hooks	Inside a second radio
5 maps/sketches of prisons Knife 3 razor blades Screwdriver	Amongst various inmates property

(II) STORAGE AND PROPERTY

5.3 Space in the SSU was at a premium, hence the storage of property, and in particular inmates' personal possessions, was a core issue. There were only two places where personal property should have been located, according to official guidelines, namely with the inmate in his cell, or in storage. At Whitemoor this additional storage was by use of sea storage containers (i.e. large, lorry-sized secure containers, as used on container ships) located outside of the secure prisoner compounds.

5.4 The cells in the SSU measured about 7 feet by 12 feet and contained a number of basic items of furniture, including a bed, a washbasin, a WC and limited cupboard storage.

5.5 It has been the philosophy of the Prison Service in general that:-

> *"Prisoners shall be allowed to have sufficient property in possession to lead as normal and individual an existence as possible within the constraints of the prison environment and the limitations under this and other standing orders."*

5.6 This principle has been set down in Prison Service Standing Order 4 which outlines more specifically what property an inmate should be allowed by right and what may be permitted, at the Governor's discretion. The essence of the instruction is that the number of items permitted in a cell should not be so great that searching is unduly hindered and the amount of property that can be stored normally should not exceed what can be carried without assistance.

5.7 Where an inmate has accumulated in excess of the acceptable levels of property, the Standing Order stipulates a procedure for handing the excess property to relatives or friends.

(III) SEARCHING

5.8 The searching regime in the SSU was expected to be in line with the wider Prison Service policy, as set out in the present "Manual on Security", first issued in 1991. In essence the following searching was required:-

■   prisoners,

■   cells, at least every 14 days,

■   working and recreation areas, and

■   visitors.

The manual text points out that:-

> *"Searching detects and deters attempts to conceal contraband, or material that could be used in an escape."*

5.9 The importance of searching was strongly emphasised in the Lakes/Hadfield Report, written in response to an escape from Brixton Prison in 1991. That escape was the first involving both the IRA and firearms. It involved two inmates producing a handgun, whilst en route between a chapel service and the wing, and taking a member of staff hostage before effecting their escape.

5.10 The report made a number of specific recommendations on searching, for example:-

- ■ Prisons holding Category A prisoners should have dedicated search teams capable of maintaining a viable searching programme (Lakes/Hadfield para 3.30).

- ■ DOC1 (the Prison Service Directorate of Custody) should review the quality of searching and detection equipment supplied to the Service. Searching teams should be supplied with special tool kits designed to facilitate the searching of vehicles and buildings (Lakes/Hadfield para 3.25).

(IV) THE REALITY OF PROPERTY AND SEARCHES IN THE SSU

5.11 Whitemoor, as a dispersal prison, had adopted the standardised 'Dispersal Prisons Privilege List', more recently renamed the 'Facilities list', agreed between all Governors of dispersal prisons. The latest version was circulated in August 1994 and appears as Appendix 'C' to this report. There are 135 separately listed items deemed acceptable, ranging from "cooking utensils" and "pullovers (2)" to "greetings cards (non-padded)".

5.12 Whilst the list itself appears comprehensive, prisoners at Whitemoor SSU had, over time, extended still further the range and quantity of items which they had in their possession. Property had filled unoccupied cells, in particular in the segregation area, and literally dozens of transit boxes of possessions had spilled over into the corridors and communal areas; at one stage this even included a bicycle belonging to an inmate. The recent repatriation of two inmates to Maghaberry Prison, in Ulster, meant the delivery of no less than 82 boxes of property to that establishment. At Maghaberry they operate a policy of allowing limited, but reasonable, amounts of personal property. The mixed emotions of disbelief, anger and despair expressed to the Enquiry by the Governor there spoke volumes.

5.13 In addition to the problems of storage and searching, the large amounts of property had created a major task for the Prison Service in transferring inmates. Often when a prisoner was transferred the volume of property was such that it had to be despatched separately. It does not appear that the full cost of such moves had been calculated but with transportation and staff provided by the Prison Service the actual costs must have been significant.

5.14 It is difficult to convey to anyone who had not personally visited the Whitemoor SSU at the time of the escape just how congested all the cells and communal areas had become; it can, to some extent, be illustrated by reference to the inventory of the personal possessions of just one of the ten inmates, set out in Appendix 'D'.

5.15 This inmate had 23 boxes of property and the list amply illustrates the wide spectrum of items which inmates had acquired, many of which did not even feature in the list of 135 approved items.

5.16 With regard to the communal areas, there were large numbers of items scattered throughout. The hobbies room was particularly jumbled and one staff member described it as

" an Aladdin's cave of equipment."

5.17 For searching officers in the SSU to have complied with the general principle set out in the Manual on Security, of ensuring that property plus all potential hiding places had been examined, would have entailed such a consumption of time and resources as to render it effectively impossible. Searches could not possibly be more than cursory; one officer explained that even when searching took place, cell searches often took less than 10 - 15 minutes each. Another officer described the searches as farcical. To illustrate the enormity of the task faced by prison officers, it took the police carrying out the criminal enquiry four days to search and log just one inmate's property all of which was physically located within the SSU and available to all the prisoners.

5.18 The Lakes/Hadfield recommendation for the employment of dedicated search teams was not implemented at Whitemoor, nor indeed at many other establishments. Although Prison Service headquarters circulated the Lakes/Hadfield recommendations, no additional resources were provided and their prioritisation and implementation were left to individual Governors. It was clear from a progress report addressed to Area Managers, dated 30th March 1994, that this was not seen as a key recommendation despite the initial Prison Service submission to the Home Secretary, at the time of the report (1991), which stated:

"A dedicated search team arrangement, as distinct from a team made up of wing officers, is strongly supported by the field. Searching would then become a fixed task not subject to the vagaries of staff availability; but there could be resource implications in particular establishments and competing priorities for new resource deployment."

5.19 It was January 1993 before Governors were canvassed for their views on the recommendation, and the reply from Whitemoor was noted as:-

"Whitemoor thought the idea was anachronistic and would be wasteful of staff. But all searching of Cat A prisoners was done by members of a trained group."

Other responses reported variable practices, but the majority had shied away from dedicated teams, due to resource implications. In response to these replies, it was August 1994 before the Prison Service issued an amendment to the Manual on Security in respect of searching. Despite the specific nature of the Lakes/Hadfield recommendations, and their acceptance in principle, no mention whatsoever was made of search teams and the guidance issued simply required Governors to draw up a searching strategy. Indeed, headquarters Custody Group specified, in a report dated 24th October 1994, that the aim had been to encourage an effective strategy for searching to be developed without insisting that specialist search teams should be established to do this work and no other.

5.20 As far as the provision of specialist search equipment, another of the Lakes/Hadfield recommendations, headquarters identified the minimum requirements of such a kit, and the prices of individual items. This was circulated to Governors with a note indicating that it had not been possible to obtain central funding but they:

> *"may wish to consider assembling such kits from local funds."*

5.21 If a dedicated search team had been employed at Whitemoor, properly equipped and trained, and regularly used to search all areas of the SSU, the Enquiry Team have little doubt that the ladders, tools, guns and the Semtex would have been discovered prior to the escape. It is apparent that the Service had not taken the opportunity offered by Lakes/Hadfield to learn from their previous mistakes or omissions. There has been inconsistency in the handling of some of the recommendations, such as dedicated search teams, and considerable delays in implementation.

5.22 The Enquiry Team have put forward a specific recommendation about search teams which is similar to the Lakes/Hadfield recommendation of 1991. It is felt that if the recommendation is rejected, whatever the resource implications may be, the Service must accept that the ineffective searching outlined in this report will inevitably be repeated with the obvious consequences.

(V) PREVIOUS ATTEMPTS TO REDUCE PROPERTY

5.23 The increasing volume of possessions was raised as a concern at a meeting of the Governors of establishments with SSUs, held at Full Sutton on 21st September 1993. Although the matter was discussed no action was taken to curb the excesses. The Board of Visitors Annual Report for 1993 documented their concerns over the impracticality of the task of searching.

5.24 The report on Whitemoor by Her Majesty's Chief Inspector of Prisons (still to be published), relating to the inspection carried out in March 1994, (paragraph 3.55) took the property issue further in stating:-

> *"We found at Whitemoor that officers searching inmates and their cells were handicapped, as are their colleagues in all other dispersal and probably long term prisons, by the number of items of personal property inmates are allowed to retain in their possession. There has been a steady increase over the years in the number of those items, each in itself unexceptionable, and in many ways sight has been lost of the difficulties caused to those charged with the task of searching cells. To do so properly, whilst ensuring that none of the sometimes expensive*

articles contained therein are damaged, would take more time than can be reasonably allocated to the work. Often therefore searches are skimped. Long term prisoners should not be allowed to accumulate possessions in their cells without being subject to search from time to time. In our view it is better to search a few effectively than to attempt to meet a meaningless target of searching all by doing the job inadequately. Target figures for searches which are set too high, and which ignore the fact that to achieve them at all, hurried or unsatisfactory work must be done, render this important aspect of preventive security ineffective."

5.25 On 9th August 1994, a month before the breakout, a Governor Grade, who was newly appointed to the line command of the SSU, identified many problem areas which have been confirmed by this Enquiry, including excessive property. He sought to encourage more positive leadership at Senior Officer level and sent a memorandum which emphasised:

"Excessive property being allowed within the Unit - it is all over the place and is compromising security, health and safety, fire regulations, access etc. It is a collective problem that needs resolving - any ideas?"

The full text appears as Appendix 'E' to this report.

5.26 Notable by its absence throughout official documentation was any answer to the question, as latterly posed by this Governor, and immediate action on his part had not ensued prior to the escape due to other competing issues he was addressing. This Governor was totally honest in outlining his role in the affairs of the SSU during the 30 working days of his involvement, indicating that the problems he found had been endemic for a considerable time. This was supported by other prison staff during the course of the Enquiry.

5.27 Prison officers had been presented with an impossible task, made even more difficult by the strong resistance and intimidation by inmates when any search was attempted. This intimidation had even led to searches in progress being discontinued rather than risk escalation of prisoner reaction.

5.28 It is interesting to note that in Northern Ireland cell searches are always carried out in the absence of the inmate. This removes any opportunity for intimidation albeit allowing more chance for allegations to be made of damage to prisoner's property by staff. The increased chance of allegations is recognised but off-set by all staff immediately reporting any accidental damage caused, and compensation being quickly settled.

5.29 At Whitemoor, faced with the enormity and sensitivity of the task, the reality became that searches were not carried out unless absolutely necessary and even then only in a cursory way. There is corroborated evidence that searches were logged, for the performance measurement statistics, without any actual search taking place at all. The Board of Visitors, in their 1993 Annual Report, comment that:-

"The volume of possessions permitted in possession in cells makes searches within the time allowed virtually ineffective. This coupled with intimidation displayed by prisoners during searches causes us to question the procedure."

5.30 With the mass of property and equipment, it would have been a simple matter for the escapees to secrete all the items used on the night, or at least the base materials, for later retrieval. There must be a strong possibility that the scale of this congestion was orchestrated by the inmates for just that purpose.

5.31 Throughout the life of Whitemoor prison, and before, the Prison Service has singularly failed to resolve the issue of excessive property, which has equally plagued other dispersal prisons. Following the riots on the main wings at Whitemoor the window of opportunity was seized to remove all property from the landings; sadly the same foresight and resolve was not exercised in respect of the SSU. It was disgraceful that over such a timespan no resolution had been found to this important issue.

RECOMMENDATIONS - (PROPERTY AND SEARCHING)

6.   A volumetric control of all prisoners' possessions should be introduced forthwith to reduce dramatically the amount of property in possession/storage and facilitate effective searching. The volume allowed should be standard to all inmates, whatever their category.

Prisoners should only be allowed that which fits into the authorised cupboard, wardrobe and shelf space of a cell plus a maximum of two transit boxes, to be stored under the bed. Over time it may be possible to issue inmates with a large trunk, which would represent the total volume of property permitted and act as part of the cell furniture once unpacked (e.g. as a table). Compliance with this recommendation would remove the need for prisoners' property to be stored elsewhere. Prisoners should not be allowed to add to their property if it would then exceed the allowance until arrangements are made for excess property to be collected by relatives/friends.

All remaining recommendations concerning property are reliant on the above volumetric controls being in place.

7.   The present Dispersal Prisons privilege list has fallen into disrepute and should be dispensed with. Every Governor is responsible for the security of their establishment and the types of property allowed to inmates should be assessed with security in mind.

When approving specific items, Governors should be mindful of difficulties which might occur on inmate transfer but Governors must not be committed by the actions or decisions made at another establishment.

8.   Searching of cells and property should be carried out, at frequent but irregular intervals in accordance with the searching strategy agreed by the Area Manager. The procedure should be:-

■   individual strip search of prisoner,

REPORT OF THE WOODCOCK ENQUIRY

- prisoner then excluded from cell during search, to avoid intimidation,

- no other inmates to be permitted in the vicinity,

- searchers to declare any accidental damage,

- search to meet the evidential requirements of adjudication.

9. The Lakes/Hadfield proposal for dedicated and specially equipped search teams in prisons holding Category A inmates should be mandatory. Such teams should have available to them on a regular basis dogs trained to identify firearms, explosives and drugs.

10. Each establishment should be required to identify the availability of specialist explosive detection equipment (MOD and/or Police). Contingency plans should include the standing arrangements for obtaining such equipment.

Section 6: How did the Inmates obtain the Firearms and Explosives inside a High Security Prison?

6.1   The escapees were in possession of two pistols and at least 8 rounds of ammunition at the time of their escape attempt. Since the escape, as part of the painstaking search of the premises and storage containers, a number of other items had been found, as itemised earlier. The most startling items were the Semtex explosive, fuses and detonators found in the false base of an artists paint box.

6.2   Whilst all these finds are significant, the main question remains how could inmates get possession of guns and explosives? One thing is certain - these items were not manufactured in the prison. The Enquiry team have examined a number of possible sources for these items, but have concentrated upon the 4 most likely scenarios, namely that the items were:-

(i)   brought in by personal visitors,

(ii)   brought in by staff or officials,

(iii) brought in by the inmate, (in personal property on arrival), or

(iv) built into the fabric of the prison at construction stage.

6.3   Taking each scenario in turn it is important to measure the reality of procedures at Whitemoor against what should have been happening, according to the rules and instructions.

(I)   ITEMS BROUGHT IN BY PERSONAL VISITORS

6.4   The most logical, and most available, way to get items into prison was to have a visitor smuggle them in. All family and social visitors to Category A prisoners were subject to the conditions of the Approved Visitors Scheme (AVS), which provided for vetting of potential visitors and provision of photographs, to check their identity on arrival at the prison. It was intended, through this scheme, to minimise the security risk posed by the visits.

6.5   In addition to the AVS, Exceptional Risk and High Risk inmates were also subject to High Risk Visits arrangements (HRV). These arrangements have been incorporated in the Manual on Security and require a 'rub-down' search of all visitors to inmates subject to high risk visits, i.e. a thorough search involving emptying of all pockets and fully rubbing down, head to toe, over normal clothing.

6.6   If a visitor should refuse to be searched, a "closed visit" (i.e. one behind full screens with no physical contact) could be imposed, or entry could be refused.

6.7   The Manual also required that:-

■   visitors left hand luggage outside the visits room,

■   no food was taken in,

■   all inmates receiving visits were subject to a strip
search and change into 'sterile' clothes, and

■   each visit was supervised by an officer in sight and hearing.

(a)   Searching at the gatehouse

6.8   SSU visitors reported to the main gate, along with visitors to prisoners
located on other wings, and were subject to a search procedure. The staff at
the main gate had available to them an electronic 'portal', for people to walk
through, hand-held wands for closer body searching and a static machine for
x-ray examination of baggage. The area used was just inside the main entrance
and space was severely limited.

6.9   On an average weekday around 20 visitors passed through the gatehouse
search within 45 minutes (1300-1345). At weekends this number increased
significantly and could be as many as 50. There were only a limited number of
staff available at the search area, normally 2 officers plus one auxiliary. The
reality was, therefore, that due to staffing levels and limited space availability
all the search procedures were not carried out, in an attempt to speed the
passage of the visitor. It was customary for inmates to complain bitterly if they
did not get their full 2 hour visit.

6.10   Staff deployed to this task also reported concern over the siting and
therefore effectiveness of the x-ray equipment provided and their level of
training on its use. Clearly the equipment had to be sited at the entrance to
the prison but the original design of Whitemoor provided totally inadequate
space for such facilities. These limitations were obvious to anyone. Certainly
the equipment was no less sophisticated than the basic equipment used at
airports. Whilst acting as an aid, few people would say that such equipment is
infallible and the 'hit' rate for finding items would be no better than that
experienced at airports. There is, however, an added advantage at airports in
that, to be of any threat to specific aircraft, any explosives smuggled onto an
aeroplane must be accompanied by other bomb components and hence would
be relatively bulky. In the case of the prison, much smaller amounts of
substance, and individual component parts, could be hidden to provide the
materials for later construction of a device.

6.11   Officers stated that many 'positive indications' on the portals were
explained away as belt buckles, or pipes beneath the floor or similarly
dismissed and no further check carried out. The Enquiry Team reported
variable efficiency in the standards of searching. There were problems locating
metallic objects in their possession and it was clear that staff were unable to

maintain full observation on even small numbers of visitors passing through the search procedure.

6.12 In respect of training, one officer explained that she attended a 2 day course at Heathrow Airport and felt the training was interesting but inadequate. On return to the prison this officer found that the "instructor" at Whitemoor had only attended the same 2 day course. There were, apparently, regular problems finding enough staff to work the machines who had had any training at all, a fact which was confirmed when Team members were searched on entry by an officer who in interview immediately afterwards admitted he was totally untrained.

6.13 Even some of the trained staff expressed confusion or doubt as to their powers to deal with anyone who declined the search or where items were discovered. This had particular significance in respect of SSU visitors as there had been a history of such visitors objecting very strongly to 'rub-down' searching and the policy and management instructions had varied substantially even throughout the lifetime of Whitemoor. Often the only check had been using the x-ray equipment and metal detectors.

(b)   the issue of 'rub-down' searching of visitors-

6.14 The 'rub-down' searching of visitors was a burning issue throughout the short lifetime of the Unit. When the SSU was opened, on the 17th January 1992, it housed six SSU inmates from Leicester on a temporary basis whilst the premises at Leicester were renovated. Two days later, 19th January 1992, a female visitor to one of the inmates complained very strongly about being requested to submit to a 'rub-down' search before her visit. This complaint caused the prisoner in question to protest that such searches had not been the practice at Leicester. The prisoners in the SSU consequently became difficult and would not return to their cells, later threatening to damage the Unit and also threatening the staff.

6.15 In the light of the threats from the prisoners the Governor suspended the 'rub-down' searches for the SSU and consulted the Home Office Prison Department. Ministers were not informed at that time.

6.16 It transpired that 'rub-down' searching at the SSUs at Leicester and Full Sutton prison (near York) was not taking place although such procedure was routine at Parkhurst, Isle of Wight, where all visitors to the SSU, and other Category 'A' prisoners, were properly searched.

6.17 Such deliberations resulted in a reaffirmation of the policy specified in the Manual on Security issued in December 1991, as it was considered that 'rub-down' searching was a necessary security procedure especially for visits to SSU inmates. It was decided that the proper procedures would be applied uniformly to visitors to all exceptional escape risk prisoners from 9th March 1992.

6.18 Three weeks after the suspension, although this matter was now a fait accompli, the then Minister of State was told of the background of this incident and the action being taken in view of the potential for violent prisoner reaction.

6.19 To coincide with the reintroduction, at the insistence of the relevant Governors, it was decided to write to SSU prisoners and their approved visitors giving them notice that the 'rub down' search procedures would be enforced. Such written notice to inmates appears to be an accepted practice within the Service. Having taken the decision to write, however, it should not have taken much foresight to realise that this would provoke further protest. Such anticipation should have included the resolve to implement already agreed practices irrespective of whatever protest occurred.

6.20 As soon as the inmates received the correspondence strong protests ensued. A senior civil servant from the Directorate of Custody at the Prison Department visited both Whitemoor and Full Sutton and discussed the problem with the 14 inmates at the two establishments. Arguments were put forward by the prisoners that the non searching of visitors had never been abused. It appears that this argument was persuasive and the threat by this small number of isolated prisoners was compelling.

6.21 On the 6th March 1992, three days before the agreed date for enforcing the rules, the implementation of the additional measures at Full Sutton and Whitemoor was suspended pending further consideration of alternative courses of action. It was thought that the search procedures might bring more trouble than they were worth. The same Minister was informed and she accepted the postponement on the premise that a thorough review of the procedures operating in all SSUs would be undertaken with a view to formulating measures which would both satisfy security concerns and avoid any unnecessary disruption.

6.22 Part of the assurance given to the Minister was that

> *"In the interim, it has been made clear to the prisoners that* any
> visitor *to the establishment is* liable *to be asked to consent to a rub-*
> *down search in the interests of security at the time."*

6.23 There then ensued an unacceptable and inordinate delay on such a potentially important issue. In the months that followed the matter was addressed in a variety of ways and obvious attempts were made to find a compromise which would take account of what was thought to be the doubtful efficacy of 'rub-down' searching. It appears that too much reliance was placed on the procedure of prisoners being strip searched and dressed in 'sterile' clothing before a visit, with the procedure reversed after such a meeting, coupled with prison officer supervision. In fact neither procedure was being applied consistently.

6.24 This situation was allowed to continue despite representation on 20th March 1992 from the Board of Visitors at Full Sutton, one of the affected prisons, stating:-

"Following your visit to the SSU HMP Full Sutton on 5 March 1992. The BOV member reported to the members at their monthly meeting the discussion held with the inmates regarding rub-down search of visitors.

At this meeting the Governor informed us that the instruction to perform 'rub-down' searches on visitors to the SSU had been suspended meantime; and is to be under further discussion.

The Full Sutton Board of Visitors instructs me to inform you that we feel strongly that 'rub-down' searches should be performed on all visitors to SSU inmates. To remove the claim that SSU visitors are being singled out, perhaps this could be carried out on all high risk inmates visitors; and staff ensure that the searches are carried out discreetly i.e. not within sight of the visits area.

Although the inmates in the SSU claim the present system has not been abused since the unit opened the BOV consider such searches to be a useful deterrent which must be practiced. The adverse publicity generated by any future abuse will be doubly difficult to counter - if elementary precautions have not been taken."

6.25 There was additionally a memorandum in July 1992 from the Governor of Parkhurst who challenged the need for the Service to make any changes on this issue pointing out that 'rub-down' searches had already been effective in finding weapons on visitors. He made the point that any visitor could bring weapons or explosives into a prison and that searching of prisoners before and after visits would not prevent such items coming within the secure perimeter where they could be used for hostage taking, aiding an escape etc. 'Rub-down' searching was continued at Parkhurst throughout this period.

6.26 The Governor at Durham had also reported that certain items in tests, despite having some metallic components, had not registered on a portal metal detector; it required a much closer search to ensure even some bulky items would be discovered, again proving the value of a number of measures including 'rub-down' searches.

6.27 Belatedly in 1993, the Prison Service was seeking an opportunity to re-introduce routine 'rub-down' searches for adult visitors to SSUs. The re-opening of the SSU at Whitemoor, in June 1993, following the four month closure for renovations and repairs provided such an opportunity. The fact that it had taken 17 months to resolve was dangerous and unprofessional.

6.28 The Prison Department never raised this issue again with any Minister after the suspension of searching practices in March 1992. The original Minister involved moved in April 1992 and it is clear that the incoming Minister was never briefed by the Prison Service.

6.29 It has been pointed out that civil servants would want to avoid being criticised for denying information to Ministers and that the handling of actual or potential trouble in SSUs was the sort of operational matter that Ministers might expect to be informed about. In April 1993 the Service took on Agency status, and this placed a greater operational emphasis on the Director General.

6.30 Regardless of the changes in personnel and status, it still defies belief that one complaint, which should have been dealt with positively and immediately had been allowed to develop into a cause celebre. It is regrettable that such a simple complaint brought about, in the first place, an agreed suspension of proper security practices for a period of 49 days, and overall, 17 months of uncertainty. The root cause of the problem was that the prisons with SSUs were failing to comply with already agreed and published practices. Whilst the absence of searching was bad enough, possibly even more important was the implied message to prison staff that security was not important.

6.31 It is not beyond the bounds of possibility that the guns and other items were brought into the SSU at Whitemoor during this vulnerable period.

6.32 As the Whitemoor SSU was closed from February to June of 1993 it follows that had the guns and other equipment been in their possession before the temporary closure, such items would either have to be secreted somewhere in the SSU or taken with them to their new locations. Neither option can be ruled out for there were ample places to hide such things behind large equipment and the searching and transfer of prisoners property was so poor that the prisoners could be relatively confident that any illicit items would remain undiscovered.

6.33 Of the six prisoners moved out of the Unit when renovations commenced, three returned immediately for the re-opening and two others followed later.

6.34 Whilst the re-commencement of the 'rub-down' search procedures was scheduled to start in June 1993, with the re-opening of the Unit, no written instructions were given to staff at Whitemoor, as confirmed by the local Prison Officers Association who had previously raised the subject with the Governor in numerous meetings. The result was that visitors were not normally subjected to a 'rub-down' search until a specific instruction was issued after the break-out on the 9th September 1994. However the Enquiry Team discovered that Full Sutton Prison seized the opportunity to introduce 'rub-down' searches, in April 1993, and this did not prompt rioting or disorder, exploding the fallacy behind its non-introduction elsewhere.

6.35 The promulgation of the reintroduction of 'rub-down' searches nationally was incorporated within a general amendment to the Manual on Security, which consisted of 21 pages, plus appendices, and it amounted to one paragraph which was not particularly prominent, and was apparently not acted upon at Whitemoor.

(c) food and baggage -

6.36 Other examples of concessions to prisoners concern food and hand baggage. SSU visitors have, contrary to Prison Service Rules, been permitted to bring food in to the inmates. This food had even been in the form of 'take-aways' in foil containers. Staff alleged they had been specifically instructed by Governors to ".. give food only a cursory glance.." although this allegation was denied. Food by its very nature, cannot be subjected to a thorough search and on occasions it was not put through the x-ray machine. Inmates have been variously described as receiving literally 'crates' of food, three large holdalls of food just before Christmas and even telephoning a butcher ordering 16 fillet steaks and 24 lamb chops, which were then delivered to the Unit by the prisoner's brother.

6.37 As recently as the week after the escape, frozen meat to the value of £300 was delivered to the prison by the relative of an SSU inmate and although the Unit was closed, this delivery was accepted. It was left to two Governor Grades to decide how to deal with this meat and eventually it was lodged in a deep freeze, as it was not considered possible to return it to the relatives without a fuss and the matter becoming public knowledge.

6.38 In respect of hand baggage, an officer reported on one occasion having to help visitors across to the SSU because of the 4 large bags they had with them. At some other prisons not even a handbag is permitted. One reason given for bags being permitted was that there had been previous allegations of items going missing from bags left at the gatehouse and so staff had become very reluctant to have such responsibility. It appears clear that this whole area had been part of the process of conditioning of staff by inmates and visitors.

6.39 Understandably where searching was reduced at busy periods, the most likely visitors to receive only cursory attention were those bound for the SSU, where the most dangerous prisoners were held. This situation was exacerbated through familiarity, since SSU visitors often attend twice a day, every day for a week or more. In addition much faith was placed in the fact that the security within the visits area of the SSU should be of a significantly higher standard than elsewhere, and so anything missed at the gatehouse would be spotted at the SSU. In the event, no searching took place at the SSU and the procedures were very far from being of a high standard.

(d) procedures at the visits area -

6.40 Visits took place in an area of the SSU which contained two visits rooms, a toilet and a room for strip searching the inmates. The general visits area was covered by CCTV cameras, but not the individual rooms within. The sketch below shows how the rooms were set out and the route in for the inmates and visitors. There should have been two prison officers present if one visit was in progress or three if both rooms were in use.

6.41 Inmates should have gone through a process where they were strip searched and changed into a completely sterile set of clothing, before being allowed in contact with their visitors. In fact this often did not happen; one officer described the actual practice as being:-

"The prisoner arrives at the visits area with another set of his own clothes. Neither he nor the clothes are searched. He then changes into the second set of clothes. Only outer clothes are changed, not underpants. The clothes are seen to be put on a table, but the prisoner himself is not watched. At the end of the visit he replaces the first set of clothes and again is not searched or watched. The officers are told to keep to the side of the cubicle only.."

6.42 The changing of clothes had, over time, turned from a security measure to a combination of nuisance and a ritual, aimed more at 'looking one's best' for the visitors. The officers appeared to have forgotten the security origins of the procedure.

6.43 In addition inmates were allowed access to the visits rooms the day before to prepare them, by setting out photographs and personal items. The rooms were not then subject of a search.

6.44 During visits, officers should have monitored visually and audibly. Originally it was envisaged that one officer would be in the visits room but this was changed to being immediately outside the rooms. In fact they normally sat together at the end of the main area, rather than looking into the visits rooms or maintaining mobility. New staff had been told by colleagues to-

"..sit down and not move about, as the prisoners don't like it.."

6.45 The original design specification of the SSU envisaged cameras actually within the visits rooms; in fact cameras and sound recording equipment were not installed into the actual rooms, following what was felt to have been an unsuccessful pilot scheme in another prison. This left the two cameras in the outer room as the only CCTV coverage of visits in progress, with a potential for only a limited view through the side doorways.

6.46 The view into the rooms by CCTV had been obstructed by the addition of two doors. These doors were originally removed for the benefit of CCTV but were replaced during the Leicester relocation period in response to prisoner protests for privacy. When Leicester staff left, the doors were removed again and this sparked further prisoner protests. The decision was taken by Whitemoor to replace them again, after consultation with headquarters for advice on practice at other SSUs. At the time of the escape three doors were in place and posters had been placed over the windows of the end doors to further obscure observation.

6.47 Due to the normal positioning of staff, at the table at the end of the corridor, they had only been able to see inmates and visitors when they emerged from the rooms. Unrestricted access had often been allowed to the

Visitors Section

Key

1. Visitors Entrance
2. Strip Search Room
3. Prisoners Entrance
4. Cameras

same toilet for both inmates and visitors without any subsequent checks for items deposited or collected. This bad practice was evidenced by a CCTV video of two visits just days before the escape (on 4th and 6th September 1994).

6.48 In the first visit filmed, the inmate and his visitors were given unrestricted access to the same toilet, without any checks being made for items being left or recovered. They were left in the visits room unmonitored by staff and at the end of the visit the inmate was allowed to take various items away from the room, unchecked, back into the SSU.

6.49 The second visit revealed the inmate making two journeys between the visits area and the cell block during the course of the visit, on one occasion he apparently collected papers in a box or briefcase and on the other he returned with what appeared to be a bulging briefcase. On neither occasion were the inmate or the items he carried searched. The officers on duty in the visits area were both female which prohibited any bodily search of the prisoner. At the end of the visit he was allowed to carry out his property totally unchecked.

6.50 During visits generally, in addition to consuming the food brought in by visitors, it had become practice for inmates to provide food for their visitors and entertainment, in the form of TV and videos, to occupy any children. Inmates receiving visits had been allowed to bring prepared food in unchecked and to transport TV and video back and forth similarly without searches taking place. Other inmates had been allowed to bring food in and to take out dirty foil containers and crockery, during visits, again totally unsearched. On a number of occasions they had stayed in the room for up to half an hour, effectively unofficially 'sharing' a visit.

6.51 There had also been an inconsistent approach to searching any items brought into visits to service the needs of children, e.g. food, toys, nappies. It is recognised in the Prison Service generally that nappies in particular have previously been the vehicle for contraband, and some establishments provide disposable nappies to preclude this eventuality.

6.52 At the conclusion, once visitors were safely away from the Unit, the final breach of procedures generally occurred when staff failed to search the entire area and allowed the inmates themselves to clean up. They used "their" vacuum cleaner, which they later emptied, unsupervised.

6.53 The string of concessions to inmates had all combined to produce a sense of resignation amongst SSU staff and a feeling that it was not worth confronting any abuses. The situation was at such a low ebb just before the escape that an internal report (see Appendix 'E'), responding to smuggled cash and cameras having been found, asked the questions

> *"..What else - a gun next? Should not all inmates be stripped each*
> *time they leave that sterile area without exception(?).*
> *THIS IS EXTREMELY SERIOUS.."*

6.54 It is illuminating to consider this Governor Grade's memorandum further; it both recorded the fact of contraband having already been discovered, and highlighted the dangerous implications.

6.55 The video of visits which took place almost a month after the memorandum was ample evidence that the graphic warnings contained within it had gone unheeded with no improvements to security, staff awareness or alertness. From records it is apparent that the memorandum had been followed up by further written debate but not by positive action.

6.56 The situation regarding security in respect of visits was found to be unbelievably lax. Almost none of the officially designated security procedures were in use and conditioning had reached such an extent that officers no longer seemed to even consider that items might be smuggled in or out through visits.

6.57 There is no doubt that the only safe way to conduct visits is to adopt closed visits, i.e. where the prisoner and visitor are totally separated by screens which preclude any possibility of physical contact, and hence any passage of unauthorised items. This would certainly be a great relief to both general staff and the Governor, but in humanitarian terms it would mean that inmates would be deprived of any physical contact with family and children for many years and this might not be deemed defensible. Providing the series of measures outlined in the Manual on Security, and reinforced by the recommendations of this Enquiry, are strictly adhered to then it is contended that open visits could continue.

RECOMMENDATIONS - (VISITS) GATEHOUSE

11. A clear written policy on searching procedures should be available to all staff, inmates and visitors.

12. All staff expected to work in the gatehouse to be fully trained on the x-ray and metal detection equipment, searching procedures and relevant rules/legislation. These procedures should be regularly supervised.

13. Sufficient accommodation and equipment should be provided at the main gate of all prisons holding Category A inmates to enable searching of all staff and visitors to take place at all times. This should be subject to CCTV observation to enhance security and safety.

14. Visitors to prisons holding Category A inmates must be subject of a 'rub-down' search and x-ray check, in accordance with existing instructions. All hand baggage and loose items (e.g. coats) to be x-rayed. All baggage and property, except for coins for vending machines, where appropriate, to be left in secure containers at the gate house or in a Visitors Centre situated outside the prison perimeter.

15. No food whatsoever to be admitted with visitors.

16. Only property brought in for prisoners with prior approval will be accepted by gate staff. This property must be subjected to full x-ray and security check prior to being passed to the inmate within 24 hours. This property should be dealt with in accordance with property recording guidelines.

17. There should be random searches of visitors and staff <u>leaving</u> the prison.

HIGH RISK VISITS

18. The high risk visits area at Whitemoor should be up-graded to provide CCTV coverage and fixed furniture within the open plan design.

SSU

19. SSU inmates should not be eligible for more visits than other Category A prisoners.

20. All SSU visitors to have a second full search on entry to the Unit. SSU to be issued with x-ray machinery for this purpose. Exit searches should also be undertaken.

21. Accepting that only closed visits would provide completely secure conditions, if open visits are to continue, visits area should be totally open plan with fixed furniture providing a permanent barrier between prisoners and

visitors to prevent circulation. Construction and design should allow for conversion to closed visit facilities where circumstances require this.

CCTV to cover all parts of the visits area and to be recorded. Lenses to be covered for protection against tampering and to disguise movement.

22. Visits to be supervised by non-SSU staff to counteract conditioning, familiarity and intimidation. These staff will be responsible for completing a record of the visit and for fully searching the visits area before and after each visit.

23. The visits area should be further isolated from the remainder of the Unit to restrict direct access. No other inmates should be allowed to enter the area during visits.

24. Inmates must have no access to the visits area before or after visits for any purpose, including personalisation (i.e. placing photographs etc) or the provision of food.

25. Items such as disposable nappies should be made available in the visits area, as required.

26. Cleaning of the visits rooms and staff areas to be carried out by regular cleaning staff, under prison officer supervision.

(II)   ITEMS BROUGHT IN BY STAFF

6.58   To counter the possibility of Prison Staff bringing unauthorised items in to prisons, there was a recommended system of random searching. The system at Whitemoor should have followed the national directions, as set out in the Manual on Security (paragraphs 70.1-70.12). These instructions amounted to requiring frequent random searches, of all grades.

6.59 Staff interviewed reported very infrequent staff searches, with the most any individual had experienced being 6 in 2 years, and the average nearer 2 or 3 in that period. It was further explained that staff searches were always held on early shift and could be easily spotted by arriving officers, since queues built up at the main gate on the days when searches were in progress. Should anyone have been in possession of unauthorised items they would have had ample opportunity to dispose of them before reaching the queue at the entrance.

6.60 The Enquiry has not shown that staff were knowingly bringing in any unauthorised items for SSU inmates. However, it would not be beyond the scope of the calibre of the inmates to have compromised prison officers by a combination of intimidation and coercion. The procedures in place were so appallingly lax that malpractice by staff would be virtually undetectable.

6.61 In addition to prison officers and auxiliaries, there were also a number of other 'official' visitors to the Unit, including the Board of Visitors, contractors, instructors/teachers and lawyers. The Enquiry Team established such people were seldom searched. Instructors, for example, were permitted to bring materials into the Unit for inmates and leave them without any form of check or inventory.

6.62 Governor grades, the local Prison Officers Association and individual officers were supportive of a system of blanket searching of staff, and official visitors, thus removing the potential element of victimisation and the embarrassment of individuals selected at random.

RECOMMENDATIONS - (STAFF/PROPERTY)

27. To minimise the risk of coercion, to guard against unauthorised items passing via staff, and to protect their integrity, <u>all</u> staff should be searched on every occasion they enter the prison.

28. Facilities should be provided for all staff to leave civilian clothes and personal possessions outside the prison perimeter.

29. When commencing duty, all SSU staff should additionally be searched on entry to the Unit by specialist search officers; all subsequent searches at the Unit should then be by SSU staff.

30. The infrastructure (space and equipment) must be made available at the entrance to the SSU to accommodate the requirement for staff and visitor searching.

(III) ITEMS BROUGHT IN BY INMATES ON ARRIVAL

6.63 When an inmate was transferred to the Whitemoor SSU their property should have arrived either:-

■ with the prisoner and itemised, or

■ in sealed transit boxes, at a later time.

6.64 Although there is a national system of cards and forms for prisoner and property transfers, introduced in 1990, the Enquiry Team found it difficult to locate any staff in the SSU who had seen or read any documentation on the system. The majority of prisoners arriving at Whitemoor would be dealt with at Reception, by staff trained in property handling, with a knowledge of the national system and access to x-ray equipment. SSU inmates and their property were taken direct to the Unit, without passing through Reception, due to resources in Reception being unable to cope with the large quantities of property being held by such prisoners. It was therefore booked in by staff normally without such expertise, by-passing any x-ray security checks.

6.65 An examination of the records held at the SSU revealed a number of anomalies and significant differences in the way individual staff members had approached the logging of property. In some instances evidence was given of prisoners being allowed to pack and list their own property and this was corroborated by unused property seals being found in cells within the SSU. The property handling system was confusing, and it was clear that property was not always searched at the despatching prison. The receiving officer at Whitemoor would expect to check off the correct number of items against the list. Again there would not normally be any form of security check of the property on arrival. Any item or substance in a prisoner's property at the time of despatch could therefore remain there, undetected, at the new establishment.

6.66 It was clear that all of the SSU inmates had large quantities of property - far more than could be easily itemised or searched. The presence of the vast amounts of property in the possession of individual inmates is discussed elsewhere, under the aspects of searching and privileges. The handling of the property, however, and in particular the transfer of items to and from any stored boxes, is pertinent to this issue. Although all property should be logged, officers interviewed reported that:-

> *"Boxes arrive from other prisons sealed. Sometimes the contents are detailed on his property card and sometimes it will just be recorded as a sealed box.."*

> *"Movement of property from SSU to storage should be recorded but wasn't always....If any item was found not to be previously recorded, and was to be stored, it would not be entered on the list."*

6.67 Once a procedure has been allowed to lapse, it makes it much more difficult and, in many ways, pointless to revert to the correct procedure. The vast amounts of property involved also added to the sense of resignation.

6.68 When the Semtex explosive was discovered in an artists paint box within a prisoner's property in one of the sea containers, the Enquiry Team set about tracing the history of the paint box and expected that the property cards would identify when it had been moved to and from storage. It quickly became clear that the records were so inconsistent that this was not likely to be achieved. In respect of the records of the six escapees, it was not possible to decide whether some cards were missing or entries had been omitted; certainly the records as they existed did not reflect a number of actions and transfers of property reported in interviews with officers.

6.69 It is clear from the discovery of the Semtex, and subsequent finds, that stored property had been utilised by inmates to hide unauthorised items. What is not so clear is exactly when the relevant items were placed into storage; this could have been at Whitemoor or another prison. It is pure speculation as to how long such items could have been in inmates' property, which has made the task of the Enquiry Team much more difficult.

6.70 The hap-hazard way in which prisoners' property has been dealt with historically owes much to the sheer quantities involved, but even when property had been subsequently added, few officers had any confidence that the records represented an accurate reflection of what was actually in any one inmate's possession. Like so many other aspects of procedures at Whitemoor, the security issues involved in the handling of property appeared to have been almost totally forgotten.

RECOMMENDATIONS - (INMATES' PROPERTY TRANSFER)

31. Commensurate with the reduction of prisoners' property, a simplified and standardised system of property handling and recording should be established which is easily understood. Items added to, or removed from, a prisoner's property must be properly recorded on the inventory and certified as having been searched.

32. Other than in exceptional circumstances, all property should accompany a prisoner on transfer and be checked against the inventory, searched and x-rayed by fully trained staff at each prison establishment.

33. Each prison establishment should have its own unique prisoners' property seals, which should be controlled and accounted for at the prison Reception.

34. Any items under construction by an inmate (e.g. in hobbies classes) should be subjected to physical examination during routine searches. If perceived as a security risk, such items should also be subjected to an x-ray search examination.

(IV) ITEMS BUILT INTO THE FABRIC OF THE PRISON AT CONSTRUCTION STAGE

6.71 At least one item of equipment (the bolt croppers) had very small traces of mastic on them which suggested to the Enquiry Team that either they could have been brought into the prison masked in mastic or been stored somewhere inside an area of mastic. As such the Enquiry could not ignore the possibility that this item, or indeed the firearms or explosives, could have been built into the fabric of the building during the construction stage, to be retrieved at some later date.

6.72 Although this option was the least likely, a number of points emerged which meant that it could not be totally discounted:-

(i)   It would have been a sound presumption in 1990/91, at the time of building, that the SSU area of the prison would be bound to house a significant number of IRA terrorists. It would have been possible, therefore, to hide firearms or explosives in the building for their later retrieval. The financial cost of so doing would be small but the potential damage would be high.

(ii)   It transpired, in the wake of the escape on 9th September, that at the time of tendering for sub-contractors to carry out various parts of the construction work at Whitemoor, copies of the relevant plans were made available to all of them. One national daily newspaper found two tradesmen still had possession of large numbers of detailed architects' plans of the prison.

(iii)   In December 1990, a local farmer, near to Whitemoor, found 4 plans of the SSU by the roadside. A further 7 plans were also handed into police and a subsequent police search of the same area revealed a further 15. Police returned all plans to the project manager for the construction who subsequently wrote to the main contractor. Sub-contractors were under a contractual obligation to respect the secrecy and had been instructed to shred or destroy any 'redundant' drawings once they had finished with them. Rather belatedly the project manager instructed the contractor to:-

> *"set up a register to cover the issue of any further copy negatives which should be numbered to the individual issue."*

(iv)   A further copy of a Whitemoor SSU plan came to light in November 1994 in Kings Lynn, Norfolk. A 4 year old girl had been given the plan at her nursery school as scrap paper to paint upon.

6.73 The apparent availability of these plans raises questions on the overall security at the planning stage and does not inspire confidence that there was a satisfactory level of site security during the actual construction, on behalf of the Property Services Agency. Whilst there may have been checks on the quality of work, and to prevent any losses of materials, it is not known if any checks were carried out to prevent concealment of items such as guns.

6.74 The prison was searched by officers prior to the reception of inmates, but this search was carried out without the benefit of specialist equipment to detect explosives.

6.75 With the likelihood of a continued programme of prison building, the aspect of security during the planning and construction stages has an increased significance. Access to such plans or to the buildings themselves could have implications for future security. Whatever the likelihood that this method of importation of items was used in this case, the foregoing holds lessons to be learned regarding the accessibility to plans and security during construction.

RECOMMENDATIONS - (NEW BUILDINGS)

35. There should be a co-ordinated security strategy in respect of all new building and refurbishment of prison premises. This should include

■ strict procedures regarding access to plans and information, with a system for booking out and retrieval of all plans issued. Each plan should have its own unique security identification feature.

■ Regular security checks to be carried out throughout the construction, to prevent any secretion of weapons, tools or other items.

36. A thorough pre-occupation search should be carried out at all new and refurbished establishments by specialist trained and equipped officers or private consultants.

37. All security measures should be thoroughly tested prior to inmate occupation of the establishment, e.g. exercises should be staged to simulate escape attempts, hostage situations, to allow testing of access and manoeuvrability within the establishment.

Section 7: How did the Inmates breach the security measures and reach the outer fence before the alarm was raised?

7.1   The escapees had manoeuvred the majority of their equipment into the sterile area and had walked past the officers in the general association area before breaching the first barrier, namely the exercise yard fence. They then scaled the first wall and were part way through the next fence before any of the security measures came into effect and their progress was noticed by staff. In the highest security prison within a prison this was unbelievable and frankly unforgivable.

7.2   From the time of the alarm being sounded to their eventual recapture there were also questions asked of various aspects of the security response which were found wanting.

(I)   LEVEL OF PHYSICAL SECURITY

7.3   The physical design of Whitemoor SSU was the basis of the official template for future Units. Self-evidently this will require some re-appraisal.

(a)   perimeter

7.4   In the actual tendering brief, sent to the builder of Whitemoor (Property Services Agency letter 9.10.89), the following intentions were stated:-

> *".. The (exercise) yard .. to be directly adjacent to the building, with the other sides fenced by standard weld-mesh fence...to be reinforced to a height of 2.5m min. by a second layer of mesh."*

7.5   In fact the second layer of mesh fencing did not materialise, leaving the exercise yard surrounded by a single layer of mild steel fence, subsequently breached reasonably effortlessly by the escapees. The reason for the change to single mesh on the exercise area was not fully documented. There was a query raised during the design phase about the need for two layers of mesh on the demarcation fences between the gate in the wall surrounding the SSU and the door to the internal complex itself. It was agreed by PSA that these fences should be single meshed, and, in the absence of further documentary evidence, it is possible that this was taken to mean all of the fences, including those around the exercise yard.

7.6   Whilst a second layer of wire would not, on its own, have prevented the escape, it may have delayed the process or even deterred this approach.

(b)   locks and procedures

7.7   During the escape officers responding to the alarm were hampered from entering the sterile areas, between walls and fences, by the locking mechanisms and practices in place on the relevant gates. For example, in the evening after "tea", it was the practice to double-lock security gates, barring access to the majority of prison officers. Access to the sterile area between the outer wall and fence was also restricted by the lack of regularly spaced access gates.

7.8 The isolation of the SSU, within the prison complex, was both a strength and a weakness. Whilst reinforcing the image of a prison within a prison, it also isolated the staff from their colleagues elsewhere in the establishment. The nearest staff to the SSU would be in the Segregation Unit, which at certain times of the day would be least able to provide assistance, for fear of denuding its own security.

7.9 The advantage of having the rapid access by staff into the sterile areas has now been recognised and plans are already in being for a further review of this aspect. It is vital that this review is both thorough and immediate.

(c) CCTV and staff observation

7.10 The installation of CCTV at Whitemoor was planned and coordinated by the Home Office Directorate of Telecommunications, during the initial construction. Coverage consists of two sets of cameras, designated as "perimeter" and "control". The perimeter cameras provide mainly fixed coverage of the whole perimeter whilst the remaining ones are moved, as required, to allow monitoring of staff, inmates and other movements.

7.11 The coverage provided at Whitemoor was subject of a review in May 1994. This review had been part of the process of installation of a system called "Diamond". This system allocates a number of perimeter cameras to be automatically operated and targeted in the event of an alarm being activated.

7.12 Although there appears to have been no official review of the control camera coverage in recent times, SSU staff report that it was well known that there was an area not covered by CCTV cameras in the sterile area surrounding the SSU. One Officer stated that he had brought this, quite recently, to a colleague's attention but was told that

"It's been raised before and there's no point in raising it again."

7.13 The sterile area which was not covered by cameras included the area outside the windows from the hobbies and TV rooms, where almost certainly the escape equipment was allowed to rest immediately prior to the escape.

7.14 It was interesting to note that many of the staff interviewed saw the CCTV as an aid to safety for the officers; some failed to recognise that they should have also been using them to supervise and monitor the inmates.

7.15 There was a further disincentive for the SSU control staff to consider moving the camera position to monitor prisoner activities because the prisoners apparently did not like it. The model of camera fitted at Whitemoor

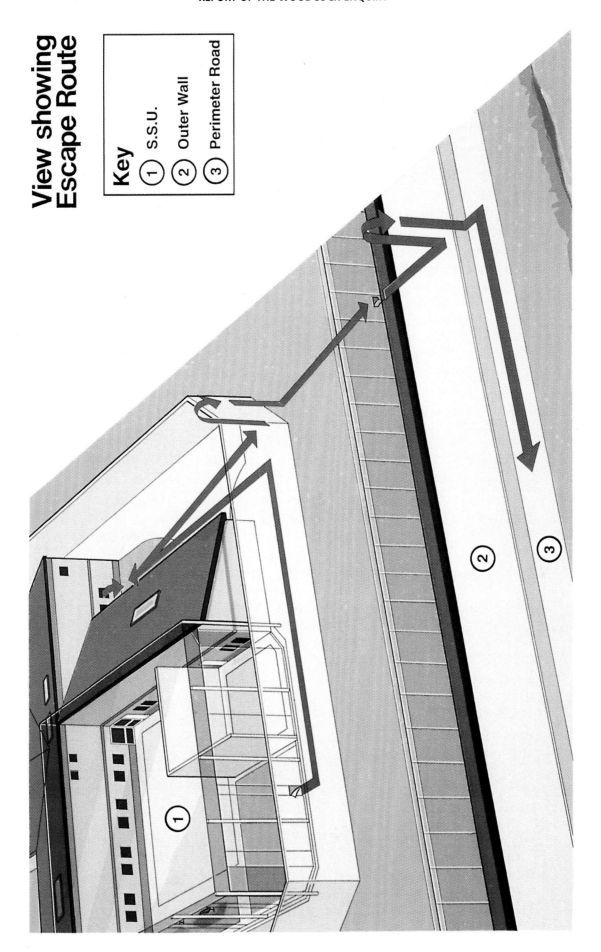

View showing
Escape Route

Key
① S.S.U.
② Outer Wall
③ Perimeter Road

SSU was such that all panning and tilting movements were very obvious to inmates, due both to the visible movement and the noise generated. Officers report that inmates reacted very unfavourably to being "spied upon", albeit they were prone, on occasion, to 'playing up' for the benefit of the cameras.

7.16 It is relevant to note that the 'playing up' to the cameras had a far greater potential significance than simply annoying the watching staff. As an example, on the 7th September 1994, just 2 days before the escape attempt and at about the same time of the evening, 2 inmates were observed by SSU Control staff positioning a string between two of the cell windows. The activity was carried out slowly and deliberately. The Control staff moved the camera and monitored the inmates for in excess of 5 minutes. Control staff remembered similar activity a few days earlier.

7.17 When questioned about the significance of the activity, the staff explained that the line, if left in situ, would be used to pass items or messages between inmates after lock-up. The officers announced that they had taken the line down immediately after lock-up each time it had been put in place. Each occasion had been dealt with in isolation and passed off as of no significance beyond being part of a game to annoy the staff.

7.18 As an endeavour, the tethering of this line in full view of the cameras would appear a futile act. As a diversionary tactic, however, it would appear to have been mesmerising, keeping the camera and staff fully occupied for its duration. No staff member had even considered its potential as either a diversion or a preparatory act in some other larger plan. It may be that on this occasion they were correct. It can only be a matter of conjecture whether such activity would have been repeated on the evening of the escape had the cameras been pointing anywhere other than their customary static position. It is disturbing that no one seemed prepared to stop such an activity before it progressed so far.

7.19 The incident with the line was also a good example of the consequences of the absence of staff from the exercise yard. Had there been staff in the yard the activity would have been stopped at an early stage, or may not even have commenced. In the main prison at Whitemoor, and at other establishments, it is compulsory for officers to be present when prisoners are on exercise. SSU inmates had applied pressure on staff by cutting short conversations on their arrival or simply ignoring them altogether. Officers reported they had not felt welcome in the yard and the practice had become to rely on the cameras for surveillance. The CCTV appears to have become a poor replacement for staff patrolling, rather than simply an aid.

7.20 The conditioning of some staff to refrain from moving the control cameras also illustrates the level of intimidation exercised by the inmates. They were fully aware that staff in control of the cameras were SSU staff and thus were able to challenge them personally, the next time they were on general duties. It is easy to sympathise with officers who knew they would be working alongside such violent men for many months. The lack of vigilance generally displayed by staff owed much to the intimidation, conditioning and underlying desire to avoid any confrontation.

7.21 It had even been noticed by staff that, in the weeks leading up to the escape, the inmates were spending more time exercising; nothing was committed to paper or even considered to have security implications.

7.22 It is difficult to believe that vigilance and surveillance could have reached any lower standards than were exhibited on the day of the escape; the pity is that this would appear to have been the norm rather than a momentary lapse. One officer described the situation thus:-

> *"Usually around 8 p.m. each evening in the SSU the staff are clock watching, waiting to go off duty, so they're finishing their game of cards, scrabble or pool."*

7.23 The value of a separate control room within the SSU was questionable because the functions could have been carried out from the ECR, as happened at night and weekends. The Chief Inspector of Prisons and Governor Grades had recommended such a change but the Prison Officers Association had resisted believing it could have resulted in reduced staffing levels. Such a change would have reduced the opportunities for intimidation and provided an additional means of supervision for senior managers.

RECOMMENDATIONS - (PHYSICAL SECURITY)

38. The review of security at Whitemoor, carried out by the Prison Service following the events of 9.9.94, should be implemented immediately. Any additional or amended measures at the SSU should form part of any recommendations for future SSU construction and be implemented, as necessary, at other SSUs within the Prison Service.

39. There should be a review of contingency planning with particular reference to facilitating the rapid deployment of staff and emergency services inside and on the perimeter of the prison when serious incidents occur or are anticipated.

40. The location and type of CCTV cameras used should be reviewed, with a view to providing a more effective and comprehensive coverage, including light sensitivity, in particular eliminating "blind spots", and making their operation less obvious.

41. Inmates should not be permitted into the exercise yard without staff being present to provide supervision.

42. To remove the opportunity for intimidation of control staff the functions presently carried out in the SSU control room should be transferred permanently to the ECR with the necessary personnel allowing the continuous CCTV

monitoring of inmates with any unusual patterns of activity reported to the Senior Officer and actioned.

43.   Inmates should be totally excluded from the staff areas of the Unit, unless invited in for specific and exceptional reasons.

44.   Immediate line managers with responsibility for the SSU, including the Duty Governor, should visit the Unit and walk through all areas at least on a daily basis, completing the Occurrence Book to record their visit, its duration and details of decisions made. The Head of

Operations and Prison Governor should also visit frequently. A matrix of supervisory visits should be produced monthly to the Prison Governor. Additionally, the CCTV monitoring facilities in the ECR should be regularly utilised to monitor practices.

45.   The senior officer on each shift should be required to keep a daily record of observations about each individual prisoner within the Unit, reporting attitudes, trends and activities. Security information reports (SIRs) should be submitted, as appropriate.

(II)   USE OF DOGS AND PATROLS

(a)   general deployment

7.24   The general deployment and use of dogs and handlers is set out in the dog handlers' handbook, issued at the conclusion of their 8 week training course. Individual prisons, however, vary the specific deployment, depending on local circumstances.

7.25   Although Governors have authority to deploy the dogs within the wings as a deterrent, it had not been the practice at Whitemoor to carry out any general patrols inside the prison buildings. There was a general rule that dogs would always be on leads and should not go within 8 feet of any prisoner. The final decision on releasing dogs from their leads rests with the handler.

7.26   It is impossible to evaluate fully the deterrent effect of dogs but they provide a versatile resource, both in preventive and reactive terms, and a boost to the confidence and morale of officers deployed in dangerous situations. In a recent example of their effectiveness, the Governor deployed a dog patrol in the Segregation Unit following a spate of serious woundings; the problems ceased immediately.

7.27   Whitemoor had 22 dog handlers, including one Senior Officer. They worked in two teams, but had a shift pattern to provide 4 officers on each of the early and late shifts, Monday - Friday, and 3 at all other times, including the night shifts. They patrolled independently within the prison confines covering all open spaces.

7.23 Prior to the escape there was one scheduled patrol outside the prison outer wall, by a dog handler at 0700 to carry out a physical check of the perimeter. There were no facilities for a rapid mobile deployment of dog handlers.

(b) the escape -

7.29 The early involvement of the dogs and handlers at the time of the escape was captured on the perimeter CCTV, in particular in the latter stages where the escapees were descending the outer wall and making off towards the nature trail. At times it was not clear whether the response was being co-ordinated and in viewing the deployment, it might be questioned whether more of the dogs could have been released at an earlier stage. It was interesting to note that the dogs did not appear to react to the shots fired by the small calibre firearms used by the escapees.

7.30 In balancing these observations, however, it was also apparent that dogs were distracted by the general commotion and some of the prison officers who were running between the dogs and the escapees. Despite the shots fired and pepper, or a similar substance, being thrown at the dogs, all bravely maintained their pursuit.

7.31 The Enquiry Team understand that, prior to the escape, training of Prison Service dogs at Whitemoor concentrated on one-to-one situations and did not include "environmental training", i.e. training structured to replicate operational demands, both inside and outside the prison perimeter.

RECOMMENDATIONS - (DOGS AND PATROLS)

46. There should be a review of the training of dogs and handlers which should cover their terms of reference and reflect the need to co-ordinate deployment to respond collectively and effectively in emergencies. Training should reflect a variety of situations and weapons.

47. Patrols of the outside perimeter should be increased and carried out at irregular times throughout the day, whilst inmates are unlocked.

48. A more flexible deployment of dogs in all areas of the prison, in support of staff, would ensure a more effective use of a valuable resource.

Section 8: Were there other factors in the regime of the SSU which assisted the escape?

8.1   In examination of the overall regime of the SSU, there were 6 main aspects which appeared of particular relevance to the Enquiry:-

(i)   problems at commissioning stage,

(ii)   privileges allowed to SSU inmates,

(iii)   training and selection of SSU staff,

(iv)   conditioning of staff,

(v)   management and supervision of SSU staff,

(vi)   lessons from the past.

(I)   COMMISSIONING

(a)   general - main prison

8.2   A number of problems experienced at Whitemoor appear to have originated in the period of commissioning, and the early months of operation. From Governor down there were severe concerns expressed regarding the lack of co-ordination of the arrival of both staff and inmates. There were also a number of equipment omissions and failures which affected early operational activity, for example, an alarm fault delayed the arrival of some inmates for a number of weeks.

8.3   In respect of staff, some arrived with a minimum of prior notice. There were insufficient volunteers and a number who did choose Whitemoor were attracted by potential financial benefits, connected to relocation, which did not always materialise. Some staff found themselves initially living away from their families, others experienced problems of negative equity. Overall there was a range of personnel issues which produced a potential financial vulnerability and was certainly not conducive to staff operating to their full potential. Of the supervisors recruited to Whitemoor, a high proportion were newly promoted, and arrived without the benefit of any specific supervisory training.

(b)   Leicester influence

8.4   In regard to the SSU specifically, the staffing situation was even more complicated. Originally due to open in June 1992 it was commissioned 6 months early, in January 1992, to act as temporary relocation for inmates from Leicester. Due to Whitemoor not having received its additional allocation of officers for the SSU, it was planned for the majority of the staffing to come from existing Leicester SSU staff. In fact, from the outset there was pressure from the Prison Officers Association at Leicester to ensure that allowances available under detached duty terms were equitably shared among as many Leicester staff as possible. The 'posting' to Whitemoor SSU was therefore subject to a rota, with a lack of continuity of staff, albeit many did have some SSU experience.

8.5   Staffing ratios in the SSU were 19 from Leicester (including a Principal Officer) and 4 from Whitemoor. Due to their familiarity with the systems, however, the Whitemoor staff tended to spend much of their time in the SSU control room, leaving the Leicester staff to run the Unit. The local Governor grade responsible for the SSU had some relevant experience but had not worked in an SSU and had never seen any instructional document regarding the management and running of such a Unit. There is no evidence that any attempt was made to utilise the Leicester staff to provide training for their Whitemoor colleagues, other than on the job.

8.6   Leicester officers brought with them their own practices and the Enquiry was told that headquarters ruled that the Leicester regime should not be changed. This was confirmed by the minutes of a commissioning meeting held on 17th October 1991.

8.7   Throughout the interviews with existing SSU staff, a consistent theme of criticism was that too much of the Leicester regime was imported to Whitemoor and this had prevented the staff ever taking full control of the Unit regime. This was particularly quoted in respect of the wide range of privileges allowed to inmates.

RECOMMENDATIONS - (COMMISSIONING)

49.   The Prison Service should review the procedure for opening a new prison, especially with regard to the:-

■   provision of expert advice from people with relevant expertise to support management in the

commissioning stage, which may include outside consultants,

■   recruitment and selection of staff, and

■   allocation and mix of prisoners.

(II)   SSU INMATE PRIVILEGES

8.8   The standard privileges for all prisoners are as set out in Prison Service Standing Order 4. It includes possessions, shop and canteen facilities, use of private cash, hobbies and activities, clothing and access to recreation.

8.9 Dispersal prisoners had been officially permitted to have a wider range of privileges than lower category inmates. It was felt that their longer sentences and restricted regime deprived them of some of the facilities available to inmates in lower category prisons. SSU inmates were perceived to be even more 'disadvantaged' in that respect, having been additionally deprived of facilities such as working in the main workshops, sight of the landscaped gardens and access to the main gym, football pitch, library, education centre and chapel.

8.10 The underlying philosophy had been to provide a more 'humane environment' for all inmates and this approach had been extended still further for the SSU inmates. A by-product of providing greater privilege, however, had been to create an impression of pampering such prisoners, both in the eyes of other inmates and the staff. This effect had previously been described within the Service as "feather-bedding", but had been largely accepted as part of the price of peaceful co-existence. A senior Governor, writing in 1987, described that the resultant regime-

> "..consisted, according to one's point of view, in the granting of sensible regime concessions in an attempt to compensate the prisoners for the confined existence that security considerations demanded, or the erosion of staff control to the point at which prisoners ruled the roost."

8.11 Staff interviewed at Whitemoor reported a view tending toward the latter interpretation. Inmates at the SSU had systematically added to their privileges by finding areas where other establishments had allowed greater concessions. They then challenged the absence of such privileges at Whitemoor and, where staff refused to allow them, referred the matter to Governor Grades.

8.12 It was the view of officers that too frequently the end result of any inmate challenge to an additional privilege being refused had been concession at Governor Grade level, with the predictable effect that fewer refusals had subsequently been attempted, and inmates had made significant advances. The first reaction to any inmate demand had been to "negotiate"; it seems, however, that on occasions the negotiators forgot that the process should involve give and take, not just give.

8.13 Governor Grades disagreed, emphasising that a process of negotiation on demands had resulted in compromises, explaining that was the reality of how co-existence was managed between long term prisoners with little to lose and the prison authorities.

8.14 The impression of pampering of SSU inmates had not been restricted solely to staff. In January 1994, an MP wrote to the Home Secretary, having recently visited the SSU at Whitemoor. She expressed great concern over what she described as the luxurious conditions and privileges afforded to inmates. The text of her letter, the Director General's briefing and the Home Secretary's reply appear at Appendix 'F'.

8.15 The Enquiry particularly focused on the elements of privilege raised by the Board of Visitors, Prison Officers Association, the Member of Parliament and personnel at the prison, in all grades, which appeared to have had the greatest effect on the practices and security within the SSU. These were:-

a.   personal property,

b.   shopping,

c.   private cash, and

d.   private telephone calls.

(a)   personal property

8.16 The extensive nature of the approved property list for dispersal prisoners appeared to have given the impression that each prisoner was entitled to possess each and every item on that list. The logic of the list must have been as an all-encompassing spectrum from within which a smaller number of items would be allowed.

8.17 It is clear that inmates at Whitemoor SSU, and indeed the rest of the prison, had been allowed to retain far in excess of what might have been deemed reasonable, by way of concession, sometimes to keep the peace. In the most recent Inspectorate report, on the visit in March 1994, the following observation was made:-

> *"..property was cluttering the Unit and included an inmate's bicycle. Apparently the inmates had insisted that their personal possessions be close at hand and not stored in facilities within the main prison. This demand had been acceded to. Indeed there seemed to be few demands that had not."*

8.18 The detrimental effect of such large quantities of property on searching and security has been discussed previously; the effect on staff morale and overall control had been to further shift the balance of power towards the inmates.

8.19 Overall the Enquiry found that the whole situation with regard to personal possessions had gone out of control. Although a perfectly acceptable Standing Order existed, there would appear to have been a disregard of many of the contents, with little attempt by managers to enforce the instructions, nor any recognition of the implications of failing to do so.

(b)   shopping

8.20 Because SSU inmates had fewer opportunities for creative and purposeful activities, cooking was highlighted as a meaningful activity. Hence cooking facilities were made available in the Unit with foodstuff obtained through the kitchen and weekly shopping expeditions.

8.21 SSU staff had been tasked with the collection of pre-ordered shopping on behalf of the inmates. The routine was that each Wednesday two staff members took shopping lists from the inmates, and drew £300 to £400 from the Finance Office. They went as far afield as Peterborough and Kings Lynn, distances of 20 and 25 miles respectively, in addition to more local shops, to purchase selected foodstuffs and other items.

8.22 Inmates would submit a list of their requirements by the Tuesday to the officers allocated to collection of the goods. No formal vetting was carried out on the list and it was left to individual officers to decide whether to question any items requested. The shopping invariably took a full day.

8.23 The most significant issue for the Enquiry concerning the shopping was the effect that this additional privilege had on

- the public perception of the Service,

- the staff morale and self-esteem, and

- security.

8.24 As far as the public were concerned, local residents and traders had been aware of some aspects of the shopping trips for some time. Similar practices at Parkhurst were also the subject of previous media comment. The media exposure of some of the more extravagant alleged excesses at Whitemoor had brought a great deal more ridicule to the whole system, further reducing officers' self-esteem and severely eroding public confidence.

8.25 Some of the officers interviewed objected to shopping on behalf of the inmates; a few said they viewed the task as a day out; the rest appeared to resign themselves to the inevitability. Clearly, many found the role demeaning and an example of the degree to which the inmates controlled the regime.

8.26 Prisoners had also been known to send officers to particular shops, following telephone calls direct to such premises. Items ordered from some shops would be delivered still sealed. This had obvious security implications.

8.27 From an outsider's viewpoint, it appears outrageous that 2 trained prison officers were diverted every week from supervising inmates to go shopping. Additionally, there was an entire bureaucracy established to account for cash withdrawn from inmates property, receipts obtained and any cash returned.

8.28 The importance of the shopping privilege went far deeper than just the resource implication or the acquisition by inmates of luxury items. Every week the shopping detail seemed to be a cause of immense tension. Of the very few meaningful entries made in the daily occurrence book, a number relate to either the receipt of the shopping lists on Tuesday or the successful completion of the actual purchases on Wednesday. It is clear that officers became intensely involved in the preparatory arrangements and acquisition to ensure satisfaction of the inmates' requirements, with relief when their approval was received.

8.29 One example of non-satisfaction was when an inmate threw a bag of new potatoes at the officers because the potatoes were too small. A great commotion had ensued which resulted in a supervisor ordering a second visit to the shops to obtain a larger variety.

8.30 The cooking facilities provided in the SSU were of a very high standard and far in excess of those required for the preparation of ordinary meals. It was not surprising that such facilities encouraged inmates to demand a wide variety of foods subsidised from their own resources.

8.31 To give an idea of the quantity of food involved, one inmate alone made a compensation claim for £75 for frozen foodstuffs spoiled during his transfer between prisons. Prior to the Enquiry the prison authorities had specified that all frozen food should be purchased at the inmate's own risk. There is a strong case to prohibit shopping outside the prison establishment with all food being obtained through the prison canteen.

(c)   private cash

8.32 The official individual limit for annual expenditure of private cash, is presently £115 per inmate plus £75 hobbies allowance. In practice there were found to be no cash limits whatsoever at Whitemoor SSU, nor indeed at any of its counterparts elsewhere in the country. Amounts passing through the accounts of individual inmates during the 15 months prior to the escape, varied between £550 and £3800.

8.33 Deposits of money are allowed to provide an ability to buy certain additional comforts, under the general philosophy on privileges. It has the potential to be a source of power to the holder. This power can exist both in relation to other inmates and in their ability to subvert staff. It is this potential which has fuelled concerns over the lack of limits.

8.34 The subject of private cash and associated limits has been hotly debated within the Prison Service over a number of years. This was brought into particular focus in 1992 when, in response to an Inspectorate report on Leicester SSU, followed by an article in the Times newspaper, which both contained adverse comment on excessive cash availability, the then Minister sought to have the situation resolved.

8.35 The Chief Inspector, in his Leicester report, had recognised that, whilst an argument existed for compensating for the very restrictive conditions, this needed to be balanced by questioning whether men convicted of serious crime ought to be able to spend money on themselves which they may have obtained illegally.

8.36 It is also worth noting that, whilst some of the SSU inmates were able to obtain considerable amounts of cash, others did not have the same resources and so, even within a small unit, it was possible that the lack of limits could create a conflict between 'haves' and 'have nots'.

8.37 Draft proposals for a revised instruction to Governors were put forward by the Executive Committee of the Service in 1994, but this produced resistance from Category A Prison Governors, who considered that the proposed changes, though well motivated, were muddled and likely to create operational difficulties. A project had already been initiated to examine the subject of "incentives" within the Prison Service, and it was decided to include the area of private cash in the terms of reference. Following an initial study, this project commenced in June 1994 and is still on-going, although some preliminary findings were reported back in mid-October 1994.

8.38 The referral of this issue to an incentives project team was a convenient means of amalgamating similar issues but has not yet led to any changes in practice. Identified and accepted as a matter of importance in 1992, there would appear to have been virtually no progress since that date in resolving the excessive amounts of money available to the most serious offenders within the prison system. The Enquiry Team understand that it is intended to put forward proposals before the end of the year, to establish a national framework within which private cash would be one of a number of earnable core privileges.

8.39 The significance of inmates having access to such large sums appears to have been that it:-

- allowed inmates to purchase a great deal more property (especially on the shopping trips),

- greatly reinforced the impression of being pampered,

- emphasised the extent to which inmates had 'won the battle' over obtaining concessions,

- conditioned prison officers to give way to prisoners and consequently affected vigilance.

(d) private telephone calls

8.40 In 1988, a Circular Instruction to Governors (No.50) set out the policy on the use of official telephones; this included that calls paid for by Category A prisoners were only allowed when made to people on an approved visitors list. Calls were not normally permitted for those subject to high risk visits and only in exceptional circumstances for SSU inmates. Between 1988 and 1990, cardphones were installed in Category C and D prisons.

8.41 In the wake of the Woolf report, of 1991, the availability of telephone facilities was extended to include cardphones in all establishments except SSUs; Woolf also stated:

> " *We would wish to see a scheme developed which authorised telephone calls from such [high security] inmates to their families..* "

8.42 Prior to November 1992, any request by an SSU inmate to make a telephone call had to be referred to Prison Service Headquarters and fit the criteria of being on compassionate grounds or, in urgent cases, to a legal adviser or similar official. In November 1992 these requirements were delegated to the Governors of the respective prisons.

8.43   At the joint SSU Management Meeting, attended by Governor Grades of respective prisons and headquarters representatives, on 21st September 1993, it was agreed that all SSU inmates should be allowed a 15 minute call each week at public expense, to anywhere in the world. It is not clear under what authority this provision of free calls was decided. In addition SSU prisoners were permitted to make telephone calls at their own expense.

8.44   This practice had been adopted at Whitemoor SSU but clearly there were abuses. These had been identified by the Governor, who had arranged for monitoring throughout the establishment. It has not been possible to identify the scale of the infringements because of the limited records respecting the SSU in isolation.

8.45   The wilder speculation within the media, of £0.25 million being spent on free telephone calls, was plainly exaggerated as the total telephone budget for Whitemoor Prison was only £58,000 for the current financial year; the spending at the time of the escape was within that budget profile.

8.46   The telephone concession rapidly became a 'right' and the inmates took over the organisation of a rota for making calls. They walked openly through the main staff office to access the telephone in the Principal Officer's office, and in doing so both compromised the security of the area and tied up an official telephone for lengthy periods. The scale of the additional private use was apparent from the average monthly expenditure of between £10 and £90 per inmate, with one prisoner having spent £300 on telephone calls between May and August 1994. There was an inmate on the telephone at the time of the escape.

8.47   The Governor reported to the Enquiry that abuses of official telephones had also been discovered elsewhere in the prison's main wings and a monitoring system had been introduced to identify and stop abuses. He had also applied for a cardphone to be installed in the SSU, prior to the escape.

RECOMMENDATIONS - (PRIVILEGES)

50. Work presently being carried out by the working party examining incentives in prison regimes and its implementation should be time limited, to ensure that these long standing issues are finally resolved.

The underlying premise should be that all allowances are 'privileges', to be earned by good behaviour and work performance, with sanctions for bad behaviour. The unlimited availability of private cash to inmates is recognised by the Service as totally unsatisfactory and should be strictly limited.

51. All foodstuffs to be provided or purchased, or any other items allowed to inmates (e.g. batteries, electrical goods), should only be obtainable through the on-site shop (canteen) or catering department. There should be no external shopping whatsoever on behalf of inmates by any member of staff.

52. All use of official telephones should cease forthwith other than urgent legal and compassionate calls. On these occasions there should be a written application from the inmate. The authority of a Governor Grade should be mandatory and officially recorded.

All calls, other than those described above, should be paid for by the inmate.

53. A cardphone with appropriate recording/monitoring facilities should be installed in the SSU. It will be necessary, however, to take account of the implications of cards as a second 'currency', by having a system for the regulation of their purchase and use.

(III) SELECTION AND TRAINING OF SSU STAFF

(a) selection

8.48 The initial selection of staff at Whitemoor SSU comprised a mixture of volunteers and postings. At the time of the escape the staff had varying levels of experience, ranging from 8 months to 17 years service. Two members had joined the SSU directly from the training school, with no other experience of the Prison Service.

8.49 The hap-hazard recruitment of staff to the Prison in general and the SSU in particular produced, from day one, an unfortunate situation where the prisoners arrived fully aware of their aims and objectives, and many knowing each other, whereas the staff came from all over the country. Few, unlike the prisoners, had dispersal prison experience and a high proportion were new recruits.

8.50 Although many of the new staff were asked to complete questionnaires as to their skills and preferences, either prior to arrival or on appointment, matching these to jobs could seldom be achieved. This is because in the early days, allocation was governed by matching staff availability to the scheduled arrival of inmates. One experienced officer described the situation by saying:-

> " *Officers were not given jobs on arrival to suit their preferences, skills or experience. There was a skills list on a board in the admin block which was divided up into skill categories with the relevant prison officer's name underneath. Sometime after opening I compared the*

*jobs officers were doing to their skills profile and it was a total mis-
match, very few were doing jobs for which they had volunteered."*

8.51 Since the initial recruitment to the SSU, the selection procedure had not
been significantly modified and there were still widely varying levels of
experience amongst new arrivals and an absence of a profile upon which to
base selection.

(b) training

8.52 In line with the widely varying levels of experience and preparedness, the
levels of training amongst staff also differed greatly. There seemed to have been
little initial specific training for working in the SSU and no written
instructions whatsoever. Several report having had a 2 day on-site initial
awareness course, but they were unable to itemise any specific areas of
instruction. None of the officers interviewed could remember any input on
"conditioning" (i.e. psychological manipulation by inmates of staff culture and
environment) and at least one stated he had never heard of the term.

8.53 Another area where training appeared sparse was in the gathering and
utilisation of intelligence. It was particularly clear that staff had little idea of what
to look for in patterns of unusual behaviour, or what to do when such
observations were made. Some staff reported having submitted Security
Information Reports (SIR) on particular incidents but received no response
whatsoever. It is important that staff are conscious of intelligence and encouraged
to make information available to colleagues and management. It must then be
collated and disseminated if the credibility of the system is to be retained.

8.54 During interviews it was clear that the more technical forms of training
were lacking. This was typified by the low level of expertise found in respect of
operation of the metal detection and x-ray machines. Staff reported that
training was too short and not sufficiently available. It was disappointing that
more use had not apparently been made of the course for x-ray equipment
operators available at the Prison Service College.

8.55 The biggest single omission in respect of SSUs was the total absence of any
course or documentation aimed specifically at training staff who were to be
employed within Units. The Enquiry Team found it disappointing that some
prison officers had not taken the trouble to read the history of some of the
prisoners in the Unit. Any properly organised induction briefing would have
illustrated the real dangers, highlighting the calibre of the prisoners in their
charge with escape prevention being the most important of their responsibilities.

(c) staff rotation

8.56 In the overall plan for staffing the SSU, it was the intention that staff
would be rotated, to prevent any over exposure to the Unit and its inmates,
with a period of six months being recommended. At the time of the escape
only 7 of the 24 SSU staff had spent less than 6 months in the Unit.

RECOMMENDATIONS - (SELECTION AND TRAINING)

54. Deployment in an SSU should be considered a key post by selecting only experienced staff. Selection should be based on ability and skills, with due account taken of their background and personal circumstances. There should be a firm policy for the rotation of staff to reduce the threat of conditioning.

55. Specific training to nationally agreed standards should be given to all prospective SSU staff, in particular on conditioning and dealing with exceptional

risk inmates. Supervisors should receive additional training for their specific role and should not be promoted directly into the Unit.

56. There should be a proactive use of Security Information Reports with a structured system for submission, analysis, action and feedback.

57. Sufficient numbers of staff should be trained at each establishment to ensure that all x-ray and metal detection equipment is operated by qualified staff.

(IV) CONDITIONING OF STAFF

8.57 In the Service generally, conditioning is a widely acknowledged threat to staff and security. Home Office Research Study 109 entitled "Special Security Units", first published in 1989, recognised this threat:-

> *"one of the dangers of staffing the security units is that the generally relaxed atmosphere and easy relations between staff and inmates can 'condition' staff into being less vigilant on security matters...Indeed it is claimed that the serious escape attempts at Leicester (1968) and Parkhurst (1976) both owed much of their near success to the conditioning of staff."*

Elsewhere in the same report it stated:-

> *"It will be evident that there is a real danger that staff, used to the easy-going friendly relationships with inmates and to participating in as civilised and rewarding a regime as possible, will relax their vigilance, especially if they are bored with their duties or if threats to security seem very remote."*

8.58 These comments and warnings could almost have been written specifically about Whitemoor. The staff virtually all reported a sense of boredom and an unquestioning confidence in the physical security.

8.59 An example of the prisoners manipulating staff behaviour came from one officer interviewed who explained that staff only carried out the routine "locks, bolts and bars" checks in the unit after all the prisoners were awake, in particular so as not to disturb one inmate who regularly slept until noon.

8.60 Another explained that staff did not object when inmates covered up the inspection windows in their cell doors because it was possible, by looking through the cracks around the door, to see any unusual activity or movements. He had convinced himself that the amount of observation was sufficient for his needs to avoid taking the proper course of action, which would have meant confrontation.

8.61 A third example was given by an officer who explained that when newspapers were late arriving the inmates would insist the staff went to collect them, and they further insisted that all bread was obtained after 10.30 a.m., to ensure it was freshly baked.

8.62 Conditioning is officially covered within two Prison Service training courses, the Prison Officer Initial Training (POINT) course, for new recruits, and the "Managing Security" course, aimed specifically at Security Officers and Heads of Operations. Although the former course involved all recruits the input was not substantial and, in views expressed to the Enquiry Team, did not meet the needs of recruits to any part of the Service.

8.63 Staff in the SSU were prime candidates for conditioning and yet were given no special training in preparation for their role. They were made even more vulnerable by the absence of staff rotation and knowledgeable, supportive supervision. This vulnerability was recognised in the 1989 Home Office Study on SSUs (Number 109) where it was stated:-

> *"staff have always to guard against complacency and as one Governor put it the danger with staff who are unfamiliar with dealing with notorious category A prisoners is that when they find they are not eaten alive by these fearful unknowns, they could switch off completely."*

8.64 The extent of the inmate/officer relationship at Whitemoor SSU was brought home to the Governor, who reported after the escape that:-

> *"A failure to understand what we are dealing with was evidenced by the shock and surprise of prison officers that one of the prisoners should actually shoot one of them."*

8.65 Briefings, de-briefing and regular staff meetings would have been conducive to identifying weaknesses, bad practice and positive intelligence, thereby alerting staff to the dangers created through familiarity with prisoners and routines. Unfortunately such meetings were not held.

RECOMMENDATIONS - (CONDITIONING)

58. There should be regular local training for all prison officers to improve awareness and recognition of the importance of patterns of inmate activity, potential abuses of innocent articles and improve the gathering and utilisation of intelligence. Such training should be applicable to all levels, including Governor Grades.

(V) MANAGEMENT AND SUPERVISION OF SSU STAFF

(a) local management

8.66 SSU staff, including the Senior Officers, were confined within a situation where they were forced to exist cheek by jowl with these dangerous inmates. In respect of the IRA terrorists, they were working with a group with the proven ability to exert their power within and outside the prison system. Experience of colleagues in Northern Ireland had shown that the terrorists were prepared to strike at the homes and families of prison staff. Intimidation by such men did not need to be through overt actions.

8.67 It was clear that such a close prisoner/staff interaction required very careful supervision and management. In fact, as in so many other ways, the SSU at Whitemoor was very isolated in management terms. Although officially part of the general line management structure of the prison, the SSU was left very much to its own devices and the day to day supervision and management fell to the Senior Officers within the Unit.

8.68 The remaining line management extended through Principal Officer, Governor Grades, the Governor, the Area Manager and the Operational Director, at headquarters. In practice the delineation of responsibility was far less clear. All those in the line management chain had other responsibilities which had demanded their attention in relation to wider prison problems and organisational pressures, often diverting them from the apparently undemanding SSU.

8.69 There is no doubt at all that the Senior Officers in the Unit were aware of all the practices taking place at the time of the escape. They were in the Unit and part of the daily routine. None of those interviewed, however, saw it as their role to change practices, in particular where this might mean a confrontation or if any decision could be overturned when inmates referred the matter to a Governor Grade.

8.70 All other line managers with responsibility for the SSU should have known what was going on; even a cursory visit to the Unit would have flagged up that there were divergences from policy. Some Governor Grades, for example, had persistently avoided spending time in the Unit or visiting it because whenever they had done so inmates took the opportunity to lobby them for changes to policy or practice.

8.71 Interestingly one Governor Grade reported having visited the Unit as part of his responsibilities as Duty Governor. The result was that he was challenged by a senior colleague, apparently fearful that he might have been pressed by inmates into granting additional concessions without having a detailed knowledge of the Unit regime. The job description of the Duty Governor was changed to remove any future need to enter the SSU. This has been confirmed by the parties involved.

8.72 In effect it had become the case that Governors often only entered the Unit to adjudicate on requests made by inmates. The absence of management presence and leadership throughout the prison was highlighted in the 1993 Board of Visitors Annual Report, which stated:-

> *"At times morale of staff has dipped with views aired that Senior Management do not give staff the necessary support and leadership."*

8.73 The records within the Unit would tend to confirm the prison officers' persistent complaints of infrequent visits to the Unit by Principal Officer and Governor Grades. This has been refuted by many of the Governor Grades and the record keeping has been challenged, but no evidence has been produced to substantiate the assertion. Visible management was essential if junior staff were not to feel neglected and, in the case of the SSU, isolated.

8.74 It is acknowledged that supervision of the SSU was made difficult because of the security measures and separate control within the Unit. Unannounced visits were not possible. Elsewhere we have recommended that the ECR takes over control of the security measures which would then allow external observation of practices utilising the CCTV monitors.

(b) national management

8.75 At area and national level, the situation in respect of SSU management was equally disjointed. There were 3 different Area Managers and 2 Directors who had line responsibility for the Units.

8.76 In the submission from the Prison Governors Association, and in subsequent interviews, concern was expressed that no-one in line management above the Governor had previously worked in a prison in any capacity. It was suggested that using non-operationally experienced staff in line management and sensitive policy making posts was a misguided and risky policy and had probably led, in part, to decisions that were not operationally sensible.

8.77 Whilst some unease about this situation was apparent within the Service, it was felt that this was not an issue for this Enquiry. It is right to say that both the present and the previous Governor felt they received full support from their line command.

8.78 It was reported that managers at a national level have been additionally deflected from their line management responsibilities by the perceived need to concentrate their energies on coping with the almost continuous change which has affected the Prison Service in recent years.

8.79 A further complication was that the allocation of Category A prisoners to different establishments and many policy issues were dealt with outside the line command. It is not clear how the mix of prisoners was arrived at or what input individual Governors had in ensuring that their considerations were addressed.

8.80 To add to the confusion about the management of SSUs, there has been nothing documented which sets out how an SSU should actually be operated. The regime of each Unit nationally appears to have evolved through a mixture of trial, error and ad hoc policy, made largely 'on the hoof'. In many cases discussions have been in response to a crisis or problem and some decisions have been taken at informal, unminuted meetings.

8.81 There have been a number of attempts, over the years, to set out a common regime for the SSUs. There were 3 such attempts in 1967, 1968 and 1973. The latter, interestingly enough, was inspired by problems over the question of payment for food out of private cash. All the meetings ended with the main differences unresolved and, as the Home Office Research Study commented in 1989,

> *"..problems due to variations between the units... have rumbled on over the years, occasionally (as in the year after the re-opening of the Leicester unit in 1980) causing considerable tension between inmates and staff."*

8.82 There had evolved quite significant differences in practice between Units, a fact which was relentlessly exploited by inmates to achieve the best conditions for themselves. Within days of transfer from one Unit to another, inmates were able to compare regimes and commence agitation for the introduction of additional privileges experienced at the previous establishment. The experience from Whitemoor was that such agitation could produce concessions and the overall effect had been to bring down standards to the lowest common denominator.

8.83 One example was that electrical extension leads, permitted at Full Sutton Prison, were sought and achieved by inmates at Whitemoor (See Appendix 'E').

8.84 The latest attempt at rationalising policy had been through meetings of the Governors of the three prisons hosting SSUs. These meetings had been infrequent and only occasionally minuted. Prison Service HQ have found details of only 4 such meetings, dated 27th July 1990, 15th May 1991, 18th May 1993 and 21st September 1993. At the meeting in September 1993 the Governors resolved to:-

> *"..develop a document setting out the parameters of practice in the three SSUs."*

The group had not met again before the escape and such a document was apparently no nearer formulation.

8.85 Prisoners had taken advantage of the failure to achieve a standard regime for SSUs thereby gaining a much higher level of privilege and lower level of control than the public would consider acceptable.

(c)   manuals and guidance

8.86   Amongst the documentation submitted to the Enquiry Team was a number of manuals and 'instructions' which had national application, either as instructions or advice. These included:-

■   the Manual on Security

■   Prison Service Operating Standards

■   HQ Memorandum to Governors (HQM)

■   Monthly Security Briefings (MSB)

■   Instructions To Governors (IG)

■   Dispersal Prisons Weekly Report (DPWR)

■   Security Information Sheet (SIS)

8.87   Although the Manual on Security was regarded by senior management as the definitive reference document, a POA representative pointed out that it did not appear in any formal training for the bulk of prison officers. The Service Training School confirmed that, whilst passing reference was made to the Manual in initial training, and the main subjects were normally covered, the document itself was not an integral part of the course.

8.88   The Manual was produced in the wake of the recommendations emerging from the Brixton escape and was a significant improvement on the previous document. The Lakes/Hadfield Report had discovered that many staff actually responsible for the day to day management and control of Category A prisoners had no access to any written instructions and recommended that

"A concise version of the Security Manual should be provided for all members of staff."

8.89   Lakes/Hadfield envisaged the provision of a user friendly handbook. This has not been achieved. At present the Manual on Security is being revised but will not be completed until March 1995 when it is intended to develop pocket handbook summaries of revised sections. Although one handbook has been produced, on escorts, effectively it will be 1995 before this recommendation of 1991 is implemented.

8.90   None of the circulations above cover the absence of a definitive document for the management of an SSU, which would embrace what practices are mandatory and those which are left to local discretion.

8.91   There has been an emphasis placed on 'empowerment' of Governors, to allow operational decisions to be taken at the most appropriate level. This philosophy, to work effectively, requires a contextual framework where there are clear, mutually agreed and understood limits to local autonomy. There is also a need to support local empowerment by providing clear direction and leadership.

RECOMMENDATIONS - (MANAGEMENT AND SUPERVISION)

59. There should be nationally agreed written instructions and job descriptions, setting out the expectations and requirements of all SSU personnel. These instructions should include the relevant daily routines and operating standards. Daily briefing and debriefing of staff should be carried out by supervisors and monitored by managers.

60. The Prison Service must provide a clear framework within which Governors are expected to operate. Levels of autonomy, responsibility and accountability should be clearly published, making it plain which aspects of existing manuals and national instructions are mandatory, advisory or purely informative. Disparities of practice between SSUs, and indeed dispersal prisons, should be avoided with a continuous programme of independent audit introduced to identify good and bad practice, supplemented by self-inspection processes such as recently introduced at Belmarsh Prison.

61. The preparation of concise pocket handbooks on security to be provided to all prison officers should be expedited.

62. The Prison Service at all levels must continue to emphasise the central importance of security in all aspects of activity. Wherever changes are proposed in policy or practice they should be tested against whether they add to or detract from security standards.

63. Consideration should be given to having a single Director specifically responsible for all aspects of security, policy formation and implementation.

This Director should have executive authority with the independent auditing team working directly to her/him.

64. The co-ordination of SSU policy, practice and line command should be by one nominated Director with executive authority. This person should chair and co-ordinate regular meetings of the Governors of prisons housing SSUs.

(VI) LESSONS FROM THE PAST

8.92 If the Service is to achieve the standards of excellence it aspires to, it is vital that, where mistakes have been identified, positive action is taken to rectify them and lessons are learned to prevent the same errors recurring.

(a) searching and property

8.93 After the Brixton escapes of 1991, the statement by the Home Secretary included the following:-

> *"Judge Tumim's report draws attention to a number of weaknesses and failures. There were weaknesses in security at Brixton, particularly the access to the works yard. There were also too many loopholes through which items could enter the prison illicitly. Precise procedures existed at Brixton but were not always followed, and communications did not function effectively."*

8.94 The Lakes/Hadfield report into the same incident recommended the establishment of dedicated search teams and the provision of appropriate equipment.

8.95 Whilst the Service embraced the findings of both reports in principle, the recommendation on search teams has been effectively ignored and, as this Enquiry has found, there were, and remain, undetected loopholes through which items could enter Whitemoor illicitly.

8.96 It is difficult to believe that, in the wake of the Lakes/Hadfield report into the armed escape of two IRA terrorist prisoners, any security measures should be relaxed, let alone suspended for 17 months as was the case with 'rub-down' searching.

8.97 At the local level, opportunities were missed. When there were disturbances in Whitemoor main wings in December 1993, the decision was taken to remove property from corridors and impose a number of other restrictions. Unfortunately this action was not extended to the SSU.

(b) use of firearms

8.98 One of the other major lessons from Brixton was that potential escapees had recognised the significant value of firearms in effecting escape. With increasingly sophisticated security measures and technology, the likelihood of staff being alerted to escape attempts in progress has increased. Firearms provide the escapee with the ability to hold unarmed prison staff at bay long enough to complete their escape. They also provide the opportunity to take hostages, either as a prelude to escape or to assist their passage through security measures.

8.99 Brixton was the most recent incident involving the use of firearms but there were a number of others previous to 1991, for example Gartree in 1987 and the escape of a convicted armed robber from Hull Prison in 1989.

8.100 In addition to the successful escape attempts, however, there have been 36 other incidents since 1988 where real or imitation firearms have been used, involved or threatened. These break down as follow:-

- escapes from escort   3
- guns discovered inside or outside prisons   6
- ammunition and other firearm parts   5
- imitation firearms   10
- other incidents where firearms were anticipated or threatened   12

8.101 Attempts to smuggle firearms into prisons are unlikely to diminish. Even within the timescale of this Enquiry one such attempt, at Durham prison, was only foiled when visitors were intercepted bringing ammunition into the prison. A subsequent search revealed that a gun was already in the possession of an inmate, presumably having arrived through the same channel, i.e. through visits. In addition, a further firearm and ammunition were discovered in Strangeways Prison as recently as 2nd December 1994.

8.102 Too much reliance appears to have been placed on the efficiency of x-ray machines and portals and too little emphasis on diligent searching. To prevent further guns and explosives falling into the hands of prisoners, and threatening the safety of staff and the public, it is imperative that the Prison Service not only learns the lessons of previous errors and omissions, but also takes opportunities to impose improvements with determination and vigour.

8.103 The number of criminals prepared to carry guns and the apparent availability of weapons have never been greater. It needs little imagination to forecast that there will be many future attempts to get firearms into prisons. The need for vigilance is paramount for it is vital that there are clear and well thought out rules for searching which are effectively supervised. The Service cannot afford to get it wrong again.

Section 9: Conclusions

9.1   The events of Friday 9th September 1994 were devastating to the staff of Whitemoor prison. Its after-shocks have reverberated throughout the entire Prison Service and have left many individuals deeply wounded and ashamed.

9.2   In Section 3 of this report the events of that fateful day are described in quite specific terms. Without the detailed account from the six escapees, however, some of the conclusions drawn can only be speculative. Nevertheless, the Enquiry Team believe that all views expressed are firmly based on evidence gathered during interviews and from submissions, as set out in the report.

9.3   The story told is one of a disaster waiting to happen. So many things were wrong, so many procedures and policies totally ignored and with such regularity that the escape could have taken place on any day of any week with the same chance of success.

9.4   Armed with retrospective judgement the Enquiry Team found it very easy to find evidence of many loopholes in the adopted practices and procedures. At times it was difficult to find something being done in accordance with the manuals.

9.5   The SSU at Whitemoor had an unfortunate birth; it was brought into operation prematurely, before the staff were ready when Leicester prisoners and staff were transferred temporarily, along with their existing practices.

9.6   Whitemoor SSU was opened in the wake of the Strangeways riot and the Gartree escape. It was a time of very mixed ideologies within the Prison Service, intent on increasing physical security to prevent escapes but wishing to provide the greater element of 'care' and positive inmate relationships which the Woolf Report had encouraged.

9.7   There were no written operational instructions for the SSU at Whitemoor and so a workforce gathered together from many sources cobbled together a set of practices which were then reactively tailored to events as they unfolded, whilst attempting to satisfy the differing ideologies outlined above. With the main prison at Whitemoor facing many incidents, tension was high and the SSU lasted only 3 days from its opening before it suffered the first of many challenges from the inmates, this being the 'rub-down' search episode.

9.8   This confrontation set the tone of ensuing prison/inmate relationships. Whilst recognising that the Service has to deal with an inherently unstable community within prisons, at this time the SSU housed only 6 inmates, who were isolated from contact with other prisoners. Consequently it required decisive action but such action was not forthcoming and it led to 17 months of extra vulnerability, turning a simple problem into a cause celebre. Whatever the final decision, the episode represented a victory for inmate power which was the foundation of more to follow.

9.9   The Enquiry identified two main underlying themes and beliefs which affected the whole regime at Whitemoor SSU. Firstly there was a universal belief that the SSU was escape-proof. Secondly there was a deeply held, inherent fear on the part of Governor Grades and above of another Strangeways-style riot. The ethos of impregnability lulled staff into believing that no matter what happened the inmates could never get out. When added to the fear of riot, this set the scene for a regime of non-confrontation where the prisoners were able to push back the boundaries of acceptable practice at every opportunity.

9.10   In the SSU there was an additional fear; the fear engendered by the abuse, threats and innuendo of a group of the most dangerous offenders. These prisoners had the resources and connections to carry out any threat they made, and the unflinching will to do so. The intimidation of officers, whether explicit or implicit, added to the ethos of concession and, coupled with a lack of positive leadership, produced the conditioning which led to the inept practices outlined in this report.

9.11   The Enquiry Team have been saddened to see normally hard working dedicated prison officers, at all levels, bewildered and crestfallen by their own failures. Paradoxically the events of 9th September have provided an opportunity to get everything out in the open; there appears to be genuine optimism that the future will be better as a result. Whilst expressing their own weaknesses the majority of ordinary prison officers have displayed commendable honesty, helped enormously by the local P.O.A. and other staff associations who have encouraged honesty as being the best policy.

9.12   The Governor Grades with line management responsibilities for the SSU have been open but it must be said that when some have insisted they never saw even the most obvious violations, then little wonder that the inevitable happened.

9.13   The Enquiry Team have emphasised throughout that the intention has been to discover the truth, not to act as a discipline enquiry or to identify scapegoats. It is more important to identify the lessons and look to the future. From the findings at Whitemoor there is a strong probability that similar problems exist elsewhere within the Prison Service.

9.14   It is imperative that the supervisory and leadership elements, noteable by their absence to date, should be established in the SSU at Whitemoor to provide a firm but fair regime where the 'dog' wags the 'tail', and not the reverse.

9.15   The command of Whitemoor rests in the hands of the Governor. Past and present incumbents have accepted responsibility for the operation of the prison and the SSU. The report has outlined a number of instances where the Governors had not received the clarity and strength of support from Headquarters which they had a right to expect.

9.16 Both Governors and other senior managers have drawn attention to an internal report and the Chief Inspector of Prisons report on the recent inspection (as yet unpublished) which had been relatively uncritical of the regime and practices at Whitemoor SSU.

9.17 The present Governor had been in post since 16th May 1994, just 17 weeks before the escape. He set about a major programme of work including improving control to reduce inmate disorder, management structure changes and the sharpening of operational systems. (The scale of the problems is illustrated by the incident log at Appendix 'G'.) In so doing, he had gained the respect and support of staff at all levels. Building on positive action by his predecessor, following riots on the main wings in December 1993, he chose understandable priorities, leaving the SSU for later attention. Without the benefit of hindsight, the fact that the SSU was comparatively trouble free was obviously a factor in his decision; it is likely that his belief that the SSU was a safer part of the establishment influenced his decision.

9.18 The events at Whitemoor have demonstrated that there was a yawning gap between the Prison Service's ideals and actual practice. The challenge to provide leadership and commitment at every level is a formidable task but must be achieved if another Whitemoor is to be avoided.

9.19 The Prison Service in recent times has introduced modern management practices in conjunction with performance targets and objectives, in themselves highly desirable. Such measures had taken a great deal of time and management effort to implement. Indeed it has been contended:-

> *"The more senior the manager the more necessary it is for him or her to concentrate on that change agenda. There was no space for senior people to spend time checking compliance with basic procedures. On those the principle had to be management by exception, that is to give attention to specific problems as they came to attention. Simultaneously to tackle change on the scale required and to have a high level of checking of basic procedures would have needed many more resources than the Prison Service were given."*

9.20 Another view expressed acknowledged that many changes had required significant management effort but insisted that if this investment had not been made there would have been little prospect in the future of avoiding Whitemoor-type incidents, concluding there was no evidence that the Whitemoor escape was the result of concentration on objectives and targets.

9.21 It is easy to lose sight of the fundamental principles and work of the organisation whilst concentrating on the management tools being applied. An example of this appears in respect of targets for searching at Whitemoor; these had become so divorced from reality as to have made the statistics produced of greater importance than the quality of the searches carried out. The amount of property allowed within prisoners' possession had made any genuine target for searches, however modest, totally unattainable. The statistics returned were predictably impressive.

9.22 Improved practices for controlling prisoners are at present being addressed by the Service. Prison officers must know exactly where they stand and must not be expected to make things appear to work by misrepresenting or ignoring the reality. Leadership with consistent and firm supervision of practices is essential to the future well-being of the Service.

9.23 It should also be recognised that a regime based on consistency and firmness is not only in the interests of the staff and security but provides the greatest measure of protection for the inmates, in particular those vulnerable to the power wielded by the more violent prisoners.

9.24 In the light of events at Whitemoor, the Prison Service is addressing many issues of improved security and better practice in line with many of the Enquiry's recommendations which have been tested with various members of the Service. It is recognised that there are considerable resource implications needed to implement some of the recommendations both in personnel terms and capital expenditure. Careful thought will need to be exercised in this area to ensure that recommendations are not rejected because of cost factors alone.

9.25 It is the right time to make much needed changes and improvements once and for all, even though the process of implementation will need skilful handling because of the predictable resistance from the prison population. Expedient temporary measures have a habit of failing to meet long term aims. Money spent now will probably save the need for a larger investment in the future. In particular, it will do much to help rebuild the confidence of the public and morale of staff which are essential if the aims and vision of the Service are to be fulfilled.

9.26 Changes and improvements with many adjustments of procedures will always be required. The skill is in having the foresight, confidence and courage to move forward proactively in such areas and to avoid at all costs having to bring about change solely as an answer to failure.

9.27 The majority of recommendations throughout this report have been developed to bring "poor custom and practice", which have grown over recent years within the Prison Service, into line with the promulgated rules. It could be said that what the Prison Service needs to do most of all is to comply with its own written instructions.

9.28 The relationship between the Prison Service and Ministers, since the Service became an Agency, imposes clear responsibility for the day to day management of the Service on the Director General. There exists at all levels within the Service some confusion as to the respective roles of Ministers, the Agency Headquarters and individual Prison Governors. In particular, the Enquiry has identified the difficulty of determining what is an operational matter and what is policy, leading to confusion as to where responsibility lies.

9.29 It is beyond the remit of the Enquiry to comment further, except to say that it is imperative that the lessons learned from this incident cause those with responsibility for the Prison Service to continue to examine critically the way in which it operates. Equally, if the Service is to recover from this withering Report, it will need to avoid, at all cost, a repeat of the inordinate delay and procrastination experienced in processing previous valid recommendations. To safeguard against inaction, serious consideration should be given to an independent review by the end of 1995 to establish the progress made in addressing the many issues raised by the Enquiry.

9.30 The findings of the Enquiry describe an awful story where it appears that everything which could have gone wrong has in fact done so. It would be wholly wrong, however, to lose sight of the fact that, even when the situation had apparently reached its lowest ebb, prison officers reacted magnificently to the very dangerous situation that unfolded. One officer could indeed have made the ultimate sacrifice and others, even aware of that, continued the chase and effected the recapture.

Section 10: Recommendations

Whilst all the recommendations of the Enquiry are directed at the Whitemoor SSU, many will have relevance to the main prison and indeed to other establishments within the wider Prison Estate.

The recommendations have been grouped into subject areas. References to the relevant paragraphs within the main report appear in brackets after each recommendation heading.

A   SURVEILLANCE AND OBSERVATION – SECTION 4 (PARA. 4.13 – 4.28)

1.   CCTV should be extended to give coverage of all internal and external areas of the Unit, including the staff office but excluding personal cells and showers.

2.   All curtains, blinds and obstructions should be removed from internal observation windows throughout the Unit. The size and location of windows in the staff office should be reviewed as the present arrangement does not afford a view into one of the cell corridors. Consideration should be given to incorporating one-way glass to increase unobtrusive surveillance.

3.   Officers should patrol all areas of the Unit throughout their shift, entering all communal areas unannounced and at frequent but irregular intervals. The tasks allocated should rotate at least hourly, to guard against boredom and retain alertness.

4.   All materials, tools and equipment in communal/association rooms should be subject of daily formal audit. Consideration should be given to implementing good practice as at Full Sutton who have a tally system for knives and kitchen utensils. This could usefully be extended to include all tools and other potentially dangerous items. All items should be retained in, and allocated from, the staff office.

5.   Night duty staff to make regular, thorough and documented searches of all communal areas on a nightly basis, for unauthorised or suspicious items, as part of a certified searching pattern.

B   PROPERTY AND SEARCHING – SECTION 5 (PARA. 5.3 – 5.32)

6.   A volumetric control of all prisoners' possessions should be introduced forthwith to reduce dramatically the amount of property in possession/storage and facilitate effective searching. The volume allowed should be standard to all inmates, whatever their category.

Prisoners should only be allowed that which fits into the authorised cupboard, wardrobe and shelf space of a cell plus a maximum of two transit boxes, to be stored under the bed. Over time it may be possible to issue inmates with a large trunk, which would represent the total volume of property permitted and act as part of the cell furniture once unpacked (e.g. as a table). Compliance with this recommendation would remove the need for prisoners' property to be stored elsewhere. Prisoners should not be allowed to add to their property if it would then exceed the allowance until arrangements are made for excess property to be collected by relatives/friends.

All remaining recommendations concerning property are reliant on the above volumetric controls being in place.

7. The present Dispersal Prisons privilege list has fallen into disrepute and should be dispensed with. Every Governor is responsible for the security of their establishment and the types of property allowed to inmates should be assessed with security in mind.

   When approving specific items, Governors should be mindful of difficulties which might occur on inmate transfer but Governors must not be committed by the actions or decisions made at another establishment.

8. Searching of cells and property should be carried out, at frequent but irregular intervals in accordance with the searching strategy agreed by the Area Manager. The procedure should be:-

   ■ individual strip search of prisoner,

   ■ prisoner then excluded from cell during search, to avoid intimidation,

   ■ no other inmates to be permitted in the vicinity,

   ■ searchers to declare any accidental damage,

   ■ search to meet the evidential requirements of adjudication.

9. The Lakes/Hadfield proposal for dedicated and specially equipped search teams in prisons holding Category A inmates should be mandatory. Such teams should have available to them on a regular basis dogs trained to identify firearms, explosives and drugs.

10. Each establishment should be required to identify the availability of specialist explosive detection equipment (MOD and/or Police).

    Contingency plans should include the standing arrangements for obtaining such equipment.

C   VISITS – SECTION 6 (PARA. 6.4 – 6.58)

gatehouse

11.   A clear written policy on searching procedures should be available to all staff, inmates and visitors.

12.   All staff expected to work in the gatehouse to be fully trained on the x-ray and metal detection equipment, searching procedures and relevant rules/legislation. These procedures should be regularly supervised.

13.   Sufficient accommodation and equipment should be provided at the main gate of all prisons holding Category A inmates to enable searching of all staff and visitors to take place at all times. This should be subject to CCTV observation to enhance security and safety.

14.   Visitors to prisons holding Category A inmates must be subject of a 'rub-down' search and x-ray check, in accordance with existing instructions. All hand baggage and loose items (e.g. coats) to be x-rayed. All baggage and property, except for coins for vending machines, where appropriate, to be left in secure containers at the gate house or in a Visitors Centre situated outside the prison perimeter.

15.   No food whatsoever to be admitted with visitors.

16.   Only property brought in for prisoners with prior approval will be accepted by gate staff. This property must be subjected to full x-ray and security check prior to being passed to the inmate within 24 hours. This property should be dealt with in accordance with property recording guidelines.

17.   There should be random searches of visitors and staff <u>leaving</u> the prison.

High Risk Visits

18.   The high risk visits area at Whitemoor should be up-graded to provide CCTV coverage and fixed furniture within the open plan design.

SSU

19.   SSU inmates should not be eligible for more visits than other Category A prisoners.

20.   All SSU visitors to have a second full search on entry to the Unit. SSU to be issued with x-ray machinery for this purpose. Exit searches should also be undertaken.

21.   Accepting that only closed visits would provide completely secure conditions, if open visits are to continue, visits area should be totally open plan with fixed furniture providing a permanent barrier between prisoners and visitors to prevent circulation. Construction and design should allow for conversion to closed visit facilities where circumstances require this.

CCTV to cover all parts of the visits area and to be recorded. Lenses to be covered for protection against tampering and to disguise movement.

22. Visits to be supervised by non-SSU staff to counteract conditioning, familiarity and intimidation. These staff will be responsible for completing a record of the visit and for fully searching the visits area before and after each visit.

23. The visits area should be further isolated from the remainder of the Unit to restrict direct access. No other inmates should be allowed to enter the area during visits.

24. Inmates must have no access to the visits area before or after visits for any purpose, including personalisation (i.e. placing photographs etc) or the provision of food.

25. Items such as disposable nappies should be made available in the visits area, as required.

26. Cleaning of the visits rooms and staff areas to be carried out by regular cleaning staff, under prison officer supervision.

D   SEARCHING OF STAFF – SECTION 6 (PARA. 6.59 –6.64)

27. To minimise the risk of coercion, and guard against unauthorised items passing via staff, and to protect their integrity, all staff should be searched on every occasion they enter the prison.

28. Facilities should be provided for all staff to leave civilian clothes and personal possessions outside the prison perimeter.

29. When commencing duty, all SSU staff should additionally be searched on entry to the Unit by specialist search officers; all subsequent searches at the Unit should then be by SSU staff.

30. The infrastructure (space and equipment) must be made available at the entrance to the SSU to accommodate the requirement for staff and visitor searching.

E   INMATES' PROPERTY TRANSFER – SECTION 6 (PARA. 6.65 – 6.73)

31. Commensurate with the reduction of prisoners' property, a simplified and standardised system of property handling and recording should be established which is easily understood and items added to, or removed from, a prisoner's property must be properly recorded on the inventory and certified as having been searched.

32. Other than in exceptional circumstances, all property should accompany a prisoner on transfer and be checked against the inventory, searched and x-rayed by fully trained staff at each prison establishment.

33. Each prison establishment should have its own unique prisoners' property seals, which should be controlled and accounted for at the prison Reception.

34. Any items under construction by an inmate (e.g. in hobbies classes) should be subjected to physical examination during routine searches. If perceived as a security risk such items should also be subjected to an x-ray search examination.

F   NEW PRISON CONSTRUCTION – SECTION 6 (PARA. 6.74 – 6.79)

35. There should be a co-ordinated security strategy in respect of all new building and refurbishment of prison premises. This should include

- strict procedures regarding access to plans and information, with a system for booking out and retrieval of all plans issued. Each plan should have its own unique security identification feature.

- Regular security checks to be carried out throughout the construction, to prevent any secretion of weapons, tools or other items.

36. A thorough pre-occupation search should be carried out at all new and refurbished establishments by specialist trained and equipped officers or private consultants.

37. All security measures should be thoroughly tested prior to inmate occupation of the establishment, e.g. exercises should be staged to simulate escape attempts, hostage situations, to allow testing of access and manoeuvrability within the establishment.

G   PHYSICAL SECURITY MEASURES – SECTION 7 (PARA. 7.3 – 7.24)

38. The review of security at Whitemoor, carried out by the Prison Service following the events of 9.9.94, should be implemented immediately. Any additional or amended measures at the SSU should form part of any recommendations for future SSU construction and be implemented, as necessary, at other SSUs within the Prison Service.

39. There should be a review of contingency planning with particular reference to facilitating the rapid deployment of staff and emergency services inside and on the perimeter of the prison when serious incidents occur or are anticipated.

40. The location and type of CCTV cameras used should be reviewed, with a view to providing a more effective and comprehensive coverage, including light sensitivity, in particular eliminating "blind spots", and making their operation less obvious.

41. Inmates should not be permitted into the exercise yard without staff being present to provide supervision.

42. To remove the opportunity for intimidation of control staff the functions presently carried out in the SSU control room should be transferred permanently to the ECR with the necessary personnel allowing the continuous CCTV monitoring of inmates with any unusual patterns of activity reported to the Senior Officer and actioned.

43. Inmates should be totally excluded from the staff areas of the Unit, unless invited in for specific and exceptional reasons.

44. Immediate line managers with responsibility for the SSU, including the Duty Governor, should visit the Unit and walk through all areas at least on a daily basis, completing the Occurrence Book to record their visit, its duration and *details of decisions made*. The Head of Operations and Prison Governor should also visit frequently. A matrix of supervisory visits should be produced monthly to the Prison Governor. Additionally, the CCTV monitoring facilities in the ECR should be regularly utilised to monitor practices.

45. The senior officer on each shift should be required to keep a daily record of observations about each individual prisoner within the Unit, reporting attitudes, trends and activities. Security Information Reports (SIRs) should be submitted, as appropriate.

H   DOG SECTION DEPLOYMENT – SECTION 7 (PARA. 7.25 – 7.33)

46. There should be a review of the training of dogs and handlers which should cover their terms of reference and reflect the need to co-ordinate deployment to respond collectively and effectively in emergencies. Training should reflect a variety of situations and weapons.

47. Patrols of the outside perimeter should be increased and carried out at irregular times throughout the day, whilst inmates are unlocked.

48. A more flexible deployment of dogs in all areas of the prison, in support of staff, would ensure a more effective use of a valuable resource.

I   COMMISSIONING – SECTION 8 (PARA. 8.2 – 8.8)

49. The Prison Service should review the procedure for opening a new prison, especially with regard to the:-

   ■   provision of expert advice from people with relevant expertise to support management in the commissioning stage, which may include outside consultants,

■ recruitment and selection of staff, and

■ allocation and mix of prisoners.

J   INMATE PRIVILEGES – SECTION 8 (PARA. 8.9 – 8.49)

50. Work presently being carried out by the working party examining
    incentives in prison regimes and its implementation should be time
    limited, to ensure that these long standing issues are finally resolved.

    The underlying premise should be that all allowances are 'privileges', to be
    earned by good behaviour and work performance, with sanctions for bad
    behaviour. The unlimited availability of private cash to inmates is recognised
    by the Service as totally unsatisfactory and should be strictly limited.

51. All foodstuffs to be provided or purchased, or any other items allowed to
    inmates (e.g. batteries, electrical goods), should only be obtainable
    through the on-site shop (canteen) or catering department. *There should
    be no external shopping whatsoever on behalf of inmates by any member of
    staff.*

52. All use of official telephones should cease forthwith other than urgent
    legal and compassionate calls. On these occasions there should be a
    written application from the inmate. The authority of a Governor Grade
    should be mandatory and officially recorded.

    All calls, other than those described above, should be paid for by the
    inmate.

53. A cardphone with appropriate recording/monitoring facilities should be
    installed in the SSU. It will be necessary, however, to take account of the
    implications of cards as a second 'currency', by having a system for the
    regulation of their purchase and use.

K   STAFF SELECTION AND TRAINING – SECTION 8 (PARA. 8.50 – 8.59)

54. Deployment in an SSU should be considered a key post by selecting only
    experienced staff. Selection should be based on ability and skills, with due
    account taken of their background and personal circumstances. There
    should be a firm policy for the rotation of staff to reduce the threat of
    conditioning.

55. Specific training to nationally agreed standards should be given to all
    prospective SSU staff, in particular on conditioning and dealing with
    exceptional risk inmates. Supervisors should receive additional training for
    their specific role and should not be promoted directly into the Unit.

56. There should be a proactive use of Security Information Reports with a structured system for submission, analysis, action and feedback.

57. Sufficient numbers of staff should be trained at each establishment to ensure that all x-ray and metal detection equipment is operated by qualified staff.

L   CONDITIONING – SECTION 8 (PARA. 8.60 – 8.69)

58. There should be regular local training for all prison officers to improve awareness and recognition of the importance of patterns of inmate activity, potential abuses of innocent articles and improve the gathering and utilisation of intelligence. Such training should be applicable to all levels, including Governor Grades.

M   MANAGEMENT AND SUPERVISION – SECTION 8 (PARA. 8.70 – 8.97)

59. There should be nationally agreed written instructions and job descriptions setting out the expectations and requirements of all SSU personnel. These instructions should include the relevant daily routines and operating standards. Daily briefing and debriefing of staff should be carried out by supervisors and monitored by managers.

60. The Prison Service must provide a clear framework within which Governors are expected to operate. Levels of autonomy, responsibility and accountability should be clearly published making it plain which aspects of existing manuals and national instructions are mandatory, advisory or purely informative. Disparities of practice between SSUs, and indeed dispersal prisons, should be avoided with a continuous programme of independent audit introduced to identify good and bad practice, supplemented by self-inspection processes such as recently introduced at Belmarsh Prison.

61. The preparation of concise pocket handbooks on security to be provided to all prison officers should be expedited.

62. The Prison Service at all levels must continue to emphasise the central importance of security in all aspects of activity. Wherever changes are proposed in policy or practice should be tested against whether they add to or detract from security standards.

63. Consideration should be given to having a single Director specifically responsible for all aspects of security, policy formation and implementation.

   This Director should have executive authority with the independent auditing team working directly to her/him.

64. The co-ordination of SSU policy, practice and line command should be by one nominated Director with executive authority. This person should chair and co-ordinate regular meetings of the Governors of prisons housing SSUs.

APPENDICES

Management Structure of Whitemoor Prison (Pre-Escape)

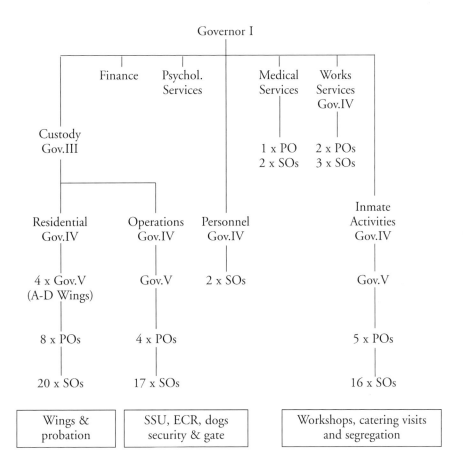

Notes:

PO = Principal Officer

SO = Senior Officer

ECR = Emergency Control Room

This chart shows only Prison Officers in supervisory or management positions.

Management, Staffing and Routines of Whitemoor SSU

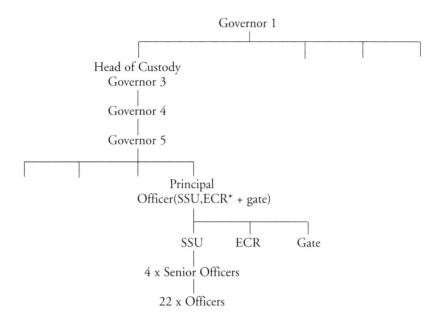

(Note: * ECR = Emergency Control Room, the main control room at the prison)

Staffing of SSU-

Staffing establishment in the SSU consists of 22 officers plus four Senior Officers. From this establishment the duty rota is designed to provide the following availability:

morning + afternoon

- 1 Senior Officer

- 2 officers in SSU Control Room

- 4 officers on general duties

- 1 officer as Messenger

- 2 officers to supervise visits (if required)

evening -

- 1 Senior Officer

- 2 officers in SSU control room

- 4 officers on general duties

nights -

- 1 night wing officer

- 1 night patrol officer

Basis of each officer role is as set out below:-

SSU control staff -

- one as "Gatekeeper", responsible for monitoring and admitting staff through security gates and for monitoring inmate telephone calls

- the second as "Assistant" , with additional responsibility for censoring mail

Messenger -

- responsible for any collection or delivery of items or visitors from the main prison

General duties -

- 4 officers responsible for general operation of the Unit, including interface with the inmates, monitoring their activities

Visits -

- 2 officers responsible for supervision of visits to inmates (supplemented if necessary from Operations Section of main prison)

Nights -

- wing night officer responsible for good order, security and safety of prisoners (locked up in cells), supported by night patrol officer

Staff work a rotating shift pattern which includes daily duties varying between 5 and 11.5 hours, with one week of continuous nights (20.45 to 07.45) every 22 weeks.

The main 'events' within the working day at the SSU are:-

	Weekdays	Weekends
Unlock	0745	0800
Visits	0930-1130	0930-1130
Lock-up	1215-1340	1215-1340
Visits	1340-1615	1340-1615
Lock-up	1700-1740	1700-1740
Last Lock up	2030	2000
Staff off	2045	2015

The lock-ups during the day allow staff refreshments, shift change over and certain security activities to be undertaken.

Dispersal prisons privilege list: 1994

GENERAL NOTES

The inclusion of any item in the list does not give a prisoner a prescriptive right to obtain or retain such an item in possession. It should be noted in particular that:

a.   The Governor has the discretion to disallow any item which he considers may pose a threat to the good order or discipline or security of the prison.

b.   The Governor advises against the possession of any item of extreme value eg. a medallion consisting of coins, or ingots of precious metal.

c.   When ordering an article which appears on the list, from either a mail order firm or another source, inmates should first ensure that the item is of an approved type. Failure to do so could result in the item being with-held.

d.   If an inmate does not spend up to the financial limit allowed in each year, he will not be allowed to carry the balance forward to the next financial year.

e.   Inmates may join bona fide record and/or book clubs which are open to the general public. This may be paid from the private cash allowance or from earnings but no additional private cash allowance will be permitted.

f.   The attached list and Standing Order 4 determine whether certain items which can be bought from canteens may be paid for from private cash and/or prisoners' earnings. It is for the Governor of the individual establishment to decide how a prisoner may pay for items which can be bought from the canteen but are not so listed.

g.   Unless stated otherwise, any items contained in the Facilities List may be purchased from private cash or earnings, and may also be handed in on visits or, sent in by post.

h.   All items purchased from the private cash allowance will be allowance free unless stated otherwise in this Facilities List. Items which will count against annual allowance marked thus (Annual Allowance).

i.   All items ordered from legitimate outside companies must be clearly addressed with the recipient's name and number in full; otherwise they will be returned.

j.   All items are subject to thorough search and x-ray examination.

No	Item	Private Cash	Earnings	Hobbies Allowance	Sent in	Handed in	Notes
1	Cassette Player Personal Stereo	Yes	Yes	No	Yes	Yes	Must be battery operated, (except where establishments provide mains facilities) - mains leads and connection prohibited. Must take standard audio cassettes ie not sub-miniature as used in pocket dictation machines. Harness and/or carrying case must not be padded.
2	Cassette Tapes	Yes	Yes	No	Yes	Yes	A maximum of 25 cassette tapes to be allowed in possession plus 1 head cleaning tape. This limit excludes cassette tapes used for educational purposes issued by the Education Department. Extra cassettes may be held in property. No cassettes may be held by an inmate not in possession of a cassette player. 3 further cassettes may be used for recording music and/or personal messages and may be sent in or out. All personally recorded cassettes will be subject to censoring. All cassettes used for personal recording must have transparent cases.
3	Compact Disc Player	Yes	Yes	No	Yes	Yes	Must be battery operated (except where establishments provide mains facilities) - mains leads and connection prohibited. Harness and/or carrying case must not be padded.
4	Combination Radio/ Tape/CD Player	Yes	Yes	No	Yes	Yes	Must be battery operated (except where establishments provide mains facilities) - mains leads and connection prohibited. Must NOT have television facility.
5	Compact Discs	Yes	Yes	No	Yes	Yes	A maximum of 25 compact discs to be in possession. Extra compact discs may be held in property. No compact discs may be held by an inmate not in possession of a compact disc player.

No	Item	Private Cash	Earnings	Hobbies Allow-ance	Sent in	Handed in	Notes
6	Earpiece for radio	Yes	Yes	No	Yes	Yes	One only permitted.
7	Head-phones with approp-riate adaptor as necessary	Yes	Yes	No	Yes	Yes	One set only permitted.
8	Loud speakers	Yes	Yes	No	Yes	Yes	A maximum of 2 extension loud speakers will be permitted if self powered for battery operation only, (except where establishments provide mains facilities). Maximum cable length 3 metres.
9	Radio	Yes	Yes	No	Yes	Yes	Solar powered and/or battery operated (except where establish-ments provide mains facilities) - mains leads and connection prohibited. Must not be capable of receiving signals outside VHF/FM 88-108 mhz - Shortwave 1-18 mhz, Medium or Long Wave. Aerial must not comprise of long, strong wires.
10	Record player	Yes	Yes	No	Yes	Yes	Must be battery operated (except where establishments provide mains facilities). Mains leads prohibited - may have internal mains adaptor but must not be run from any external power source.
11	Records	Yes	Yes	No	Yes	Yes	A maximum of 25 LPs or EPs with plastic sleeves allowed in possession - extra records may by held in property. A nylon brush may be permitted for cleaning purposes. No records may be held by an inmate not in possession of a record player.
12	Storage case for records/ cassettes/ compact discs	Yes	Yes	No	Yes	Yes	For records or cassettes or CDs. One or two unpadded cases to hold a maximum of 40 items.

No	Item	Private Cash	Earnings	Hobbies Allow-ance	Sent in	Handed in	Notes
13	Bedspread	Yes	Yes	No	Yes	Yes	Single bed size only - must not be padded or quilted.
14	Curtains	Yes	Yes	No	Yes	Yes	One pair only allowed of a reasonable size to be decided at local discretion. Net curtains to be allowed at local discretion.
15	Floor mat	Yes	Yes	No	Yes	Yes	Maximum 6ft x 3ft (or equivalent for circular or oval mats) at local discretion.
16	Table cover	Yes	Yes	No	Yes	Yes	Maximum 4ft x 4ft (or equivalent for circular table covers).
17	Footwear (indoor)	Yes	Yes	No	Yes	Yes	Flipflops, sandals and slippers - one pair of each allowed.
18	Footwear (Training/ Baseball Shoes, Basketball Boots)	Yes	Yes	No	Yes	Yes	A total of 2 pairs of any combination of the aforementioned allowed. Must not have metal inserts.
19	Footwear (Weight Training Shoes)	Yes	Yes	No	Yes	Yes	One pair only allowed on application - must be kept in the Gym.
20	T-Shirts/ Sweat Shirts/ Polo Shirts/ Button up Shirts	Yes	Yes	No	Yes	Yes	A combined total of 6 shirts allowed in possession. The pattern, colour and form of decoration should be such as to cause no difficulty in the maintenance of good order and discipline nor to be unacceptably offensive to others. Hoods are not allowed. No uniform style shirts in blue or white allowed.
21	Under-pants	Yes	Yes	No	Yes	Yes	A maximum of 7 pairs allowed in possession.
22	Vests	Yes	Yes	No	Yes	Yes	A maximum of 7 allowed in possession - must be plain, single colour.

No	Item	Private Cash	Earnings	Hobbies Allow- ance	Sent in	Handed in	Notes
23	Jeans	Yes	Yes	No	Yes	Yes	A maximum of 2 pairs allowed in possession. Must be of a similar colour and style to issue jeans and be in good repair. Cords not allowed.
24	Batteries	Yes	Yes	No	No	No	For permitted personal equipment only - one set plus one spare set allowed for each item of equipment. Maximum size should be PP9 or PPJ96. Only those types authorised by Headquarters to be allowed.
25	Books	Yes	Yes	No	Yes	Yes	A maximum of 12 allowed in possession plus approved text books. Hardback or paperback which must be in good condition.
26	Butter dish	Yes	Yes	No	Yes	Yes	Plastic only.
27	Calculator	Yes	Yes	No	Yes	Yes	Programmable or printout type is not permitted. Memory function allowed.
28	Calendar	Yes	Yes	No	Yes	Yes	
29	Games (including Spell-check, Word-finder, Gameboy etc)	Yes	Yes	No	Yes	Yes	A maximum of 5 games allowed in possession including electronic games (without data storage facili ties) if they are self-contained non-programmable units.
30	Chain	Yes	Yes	No	Yes	Yes	One only allowed in possession which must be lightweight and have a maximum length of 2ft. May be used for medallion or crucifix.
31	Cooking Utensils	Yes	Yes	No	No	Yes	3 saucepans or one frying pan/wok and 2 saucepans allowed in possession. No knives. Depending on the facilities available additional items may be permitted at local discretion. Plastic cheese grater allowed. Tin opener, small butterfly wheel type.

No	Item	Private Cash	Earnings	Hobbies Allow- ance	Sent in	Handed in	Notes
32	Crockery	Yes	Yes	No	Yes	Yes	One cup and saucer or mug and saucer, 2 plates and one cereal bowl allowed in possession. All items must be made of china or plastic/melamine only.
33	Earring/ Stud	Yes	Yes	No	Yes	Yes	If worn on arrival. Must be of a reasonable size at Governor's discretion.
34	Flowers	Yes	Yes	No	Yes	No	Reasonable quantity of cut flowers direct from florist only.
35	Food containers	Yes	Yes	No	Yes	Yes	Plastic only and of reasonable size.
36	Greeting Cards (Not padded)	Yes	Yes	No	No	No	A maximum of 24 cards may be sent or handed out at Christmas. For other religious festivals it is at the discretion of individual Governors to decide whether a particular prisoner should be allowed to send cards to mark a particular festival. Blank cards may only be purchased from prison canteens. Blank cards may not be handed in, filled in and sent out. Cards completed by prisoners may be handed out or sent out by post. Only completed cards written to prisoners may be sent in or handed in.
37	Maps	Yes	Yes	No	Yes	Yes	Maps may be held in possession, either loose or as illustrations in books, with the following conditions:-
							1 There is no restriction on maps of any size or type which cover any countries excluding England, Wales, Scotland or Northern Ireland. 2 Maps to a scale of 1:100,000 of England, Wales, Scotland and Northern Ireland are permitted; more detailed maps are not permitted.

No	Item	Private Cash	Earnings	Hobbies Allow- ance	Sent in	Handed in	Notes
							3 Navigational maps of United Kingdom coastal waters are not permitted. 4 Air navigation maps of the United Kingdom or any part thereof are not permitted. 5 Specific maps can be excluded on the authority of the Governor or the Prison Department for security or other reasons.
38	Medallion	Yes	Yes	No	Yes	Yes	Maximum dimension of $1^1/_2$ inches.
39	Multi-purpose items (eg pen with time display)	Yes	Yes	No	Yes	Yes	Each constituent feature must be an approved item. The item itself may only be acquired by the method applying to its most restricted component.
40	Musical instru-ment	Yes	Yes	No	Yes	Yes	Includes electronic musical key boards which must be battery operated with no recording facility but may have an integral memory function. To be used with head-phones. Instrument will only be allowed if acceptable on security or noise level grounds. Instruments allowed may vary from prison to prison at Governor's discretion.
41	News-papers and period-icals	Yes	Yes	No	Yes	Yes	Allowed in accordance with the restrictions set out in Standing Order 4. 6 may be retained.
42	Panto-graph	Yes	Yes	Yes	Yes	Yes	Must be of a reasonable size and of a wooden or plastic construction.
43	Pens, pencils and ink	Yes	Yes	No	No	No	Felt tip pens must be non-toxic. Calligraphy pens - cartridge only.

No	Item	Private Cash	Earnings	Hobbies Allowance	Sent in	Handed in	Notes
44	Pencil sharpener	Yes	Yes	No	No	No	Single blade - small.
45	Photographs and pictures	Yes	Yes	No	Yes	Yes	Unglazed only. Posters - maximum size 4ft x 3ft.
46	Photograph album	Yes	Yes	No	Yes	Yes	Commemorative sets of unglazed photographs allowed in unpadded albums. "Photo Cubes" not allowed.
47	Photograph corners	Yes	Yes	No	Yes	Yes	
48	Playing cards	Yes	Yes	No	Yes	Yes	
49	Potted plants or bulbs	Yes	Yes	No	No	No	A maximum of 2 potted plants allowed only which must be housed in plastic containers of a reasonable size.
50	Ring	Yes	Yes	No	Yes	Yes	One plain ring with no set stones or raised decoration, allowed at Governor's discretion.
51	Ring folders	Yes	Yes	No	Yes	Yes	Must be unpadded.
52	Scrapbook	Yes	Yes	No	Yes	Yes	
53	Smoking requisites	Yes	Yes	No	Yes	Yes	Pipe, tobacco pouch, tinder lighter, pipe cleaners, cigarette rolling machine allowed.
54	Teapot/ Cafetiere	Yes	Yes	No	Yes	Yes	Maximum capacity of 2 pints.
55	Tea strainer	Yes	Yes	No	Yes	Yes	Plastic only
56	Towels	Yes	Yes	No	Yes	Yes	In good condition. Maximum of 6.
57	Vacuum flask	Yes	Yes	No	Yes	Yes	Maximum capacity of 2 pints. Must have plastic outer casing and to remain on wing.

No	Item	Private Cash	Earnings	Hobbies Allow- ance	Sent in	Handed in	Notes
58	Watch/ clock	Yes	Yes	No	Yes	Yes	Wrist or pocket type allowed. Alarm function and/or stopwatch function allowed.
59	Budgerigar (or other small birds)	Yes	Yes	Yes	Yes	Yes	One only allowed at Governor's discretion. Cage must be in possession first.
60	Birdcage and Accessories	Yes	Yes	Yes	Yes	Yes	One only allowed of either metal or wood construction. Maximum size 28" x 18" x 16".
61	Bird Food	Yes	Yes	Yes	No	No	
62	Calli- graphy pens	Yes	Yes	Yes	No	No	
63	Canvas, Cartridge pads, hardboard	Yes	Yes	Yes	No	No	To be used for painting. Maximum size 3ft x 2ft.
64	Comp- asses	Yes	Yes	Yes	No	No	Type of compass allowed at Governor's discretion. Not to be retained in possession when not in use.
65	Garden seeds	Yes	Yes	Yes	No	No	Only allowed where garden facility exists. Advice on restricted seeds can be obtained from the prison.
66	Model Cement/ Glues	Yes	Yes	Yes	No	No	Suitable approved brands only - see guidance notes at end of index.
67	Leather and Tools	Yes	Yes	Yes	No	No	One small hammer, one light duty leather work hole punch, one pair of light duty rivetting pliers - all items to be retained and con- trolled by staff when not in use.
68	Model kit	Yes	Yes	Yes	No	No	No dimension of assembled arti cles to exceed 3ft.
69	Musical movement	Yes	Yes	Yes	No	No	To be controlled by the Education Department.

No	Item	Private Cash	Earnings	Hobbies Allow-ance	Sent in	Handed in	Notes
70	Paints and Paint Brushes	Yes	Yes	Yes	No	No	Approved type only which must be purchased through official sources.
71	Panel pins	Yes	Yes	Yes	No	No	
72	Picture framing materials	Yes	Yes	Yes	No	No	No glass or metal frames allowed.
73	Rug making kit	Yes	Yes	Yes	No	No	Tools must be staff controlled. Maximum size of finished rug to be 6ft x 3ft at Governor's discretion. May only be held as an alternative to a tapestry kit - not in addition.
74	Small knife	Yes	Yes	Yes	No	No	Use to be controlled by staff. Light-weight plastic handle, retractable or small fixed blade.
75	Small (toffee) hammer	Yes	Yes	Yes	No	No	Not to be retained in possession when not in use.
76	Small sundry hobbies items	Yes	Yes	Yes	No	No	eg. small hinges, hooks, small screws, clasps, felt lining.
77	Soft toy material (where this hobby is permitted)	Yes	Yes	Yes	No	No	Quantity allowed in cell to be controlled by Wing Office and limited to minimum necessary.
78	Tapestry kit	Yes	Yes	Yes	No	No	May only be held as an alternative to a rug making kit and not in addition.
79	Threads (for collages etc)	Yes	Yes	Yes	No	No	Single filament thread not allowed.
80	Varnish (clear)	Yes	Yes	Yes	No	No	Quantity allowed controlled by the Wing Office and limited to the minimum necessary - see guidance notes at end of index.

No	Item	Private Cash	Earnings	Hobbies Allowance	Sent in	Handed in	Notes
81	Wood	Yes	Yes	Yes	No	No	Maximum of 6ft square allowed at any one time in possession (ie 3ft x 2ft x 1").
82	Wood or Leather dye	Yes	Yes	Yes	No	No	Quantity allowed controlled by the Wing Office and limited to minimum necessary - see guidance notes at end of index.
83	Cross/ crucifix and other religious symbols including Buddhist statue and Madonna	Yes	Yes	No	Yes	Yes	One free standing and one hanging on a chain allowed - dimensions subject to local discretion.
84	Prayer mat and cap	Yes	Yes	No	Yes	Yes	
85	Rosary beads	Yes	Yes	No	Yes	Yes	
86	Badmin-ton Racquet	Yes	Yes	No	Yes	Yes	Storage at Governor's discretion. One only in possession.
87	Shuttle-cocks	Yes	Yes	No	Yes	Yes	
88	Billiard cue	Yes	Yes	No	Yes	Yes	Not to be retained in inmates possession when not in use.
89	Darts and dart flights	Yes	Yes	No	Yes	Yes	One set only allowed - not to be retained in inmate's possession when not in use.
90	Football boots	Yes	Yes	No	Yes	Yes	One pair only allowed.
91	Gum shield	Yes	Yes	No	No	No	For rugby players only - to be kept in gym when not in use.
92	"Jock strap"	Yes	Yes	No	Yes	Yes	
93	Shorts	Yes	Yes	No	Yes	Yes	4 pairs only allowed. Lycra included.

No	Item	Private Cash	Earnings	Hobbies Allow-ance	Sent in	Handed in	Notes
94	Socks	Yes	Yes	No	Yes	Yes	7 pairs only allowed.
95	Table tennis bat	Yes	Yes	No	Yes	Yes	
96	Table tennis balls	Yes	Yes	No	Yes	Yes	
97	Weight lifting knee supports	Yes	Yes	No	Yes	Yes	One pair allowed on application - to be kept in the gym.
98	Battery shaver	Yes	Yes	No	Yes	Yes	
99	Nail clippers	Yes	Yes	No	Yes	Yes	Approved "alligator" clipper type only - no plier variety allowed.
100	Comb	Yes	Yes	No	Yes	Yes	Plastic only.
101	Flannel	Yes	Yes	No	Yes	Yes	
102	Hairbrush	Yes	Yes	No	Yes	Yes	Plastic only.
103	Nailbrush	Yes	Yes	No	Yes	Yes	
104	Razor	Yes	Yes	No	Yes	Yes	Safety razor only with non-removable blades.
105	Shower cap	Yes	Yes	No	Yes	Yes	One only - without decoration. Must not be padded or quilted.
106	Toilet bag	Yes	Yes	No	Yes	Yes	Not padded or quilted.
107	Tooth-brush	Yes	Yes	No	Yes	Yes	Includes battery operated models.
108	Tweezers	Yes	Yes	No	Yes	Yes	
109	Pocket diaries/ personal organisers	Yes	Yes	No	Yes	Yes	
110	Hats	Yes	Yes	No	Yes	Yes	Must not be capable of use as a face mask (eg woollen hats which can become balaclavas) - must not be of Prison Officer's uniform type - must not be worn on visits.

No	Item	Private Cash	Earnings	Hobbies Allow- ance	Sent in	Handed in	Notes
111	Track/ Shell suits	Yes	Yes	No	Yes	Yes	Two only allowed in possession - must not be of a padded or quilt ed material. Must not have a hood. Not dark blue or black. No emblems or slogans which may develop rivalries or cause offence. Tops or bottoms may be purchased separately.
112	Bathrobes	Yes	Yes	No	Yes	Yes	Must not be padded or quilted and without a hood.
113	Garment shaver	Yes	Yes	No	Yes	Yes	Battery operated only.
114	Writing paper and envelopes (one pad, one pack envelopes)	Yes	Yes	No	Yes	Yes	
115	Hand held sewing machine	Yes	Yes	Yes	Yes	Yes	Palm held only - manual or battery operated.
116	Phone- cards	Yes	Yes	No	No	No	
117	Speaker wire	Yes	Yes	Yes	No	No	Maximum length 3 metres - no crocodile clips.
118	Toilet pedestal mat	Yes	Yes	No	Yes	Yes	One only allowed.
119	Toilet seat cover	Yes	Yes	No	Yes	Yes	One only allowed.
120	Tea towels	Yes	Yes	No	Yes	Yes	Maximum of 4 allowed in possession.
121	Pillow cases	Yes	Yes	No	Yes	Yes	Maximum of 2 allowed in posses- sion.
122	Sheets	Yes	Yes	No	Yes	Yes	Maximum of 2 allowed in possession.
123	Pyrex dishes	Yes	Yes	No	Yes	Yes	Maximum of 2, with lids, allowed in possession.

No	Item	Private Cash	Earnings	Hobbies Allow-ance	Sent in	Handed in	Notes
124	Typewriter	Yes	Yes	No	Yes	Yes	Must be manual type ie not electric, or word processor, except at Governor's discretion for legal aid or educational purposes.
125	Address book	Yes	Yes	No	Yes	Yes	Must not be padded.
126	Weight training belt	Yes	Yes	Yes	Yes	Yes	One only - to be kept in gym.
127	Pullovers	Yes	Yes	No	Yes	Yes	Two allowed in addition to sweatshirts, T-shirts and track-suits. Must not be of a type which could be mistaken for Prison Officer uniform.
128	Sandpaper	Yes	Yes	Yes	No	No	No carborundum or emery cloth. Finest grade wet and dry paper is permitted.
129	Micro-phone	Yes	Yes	No	Yes	Yes	For recording or personal messages only. Cable no longer than 2 metres.
130	Pyjamas	Yes	Yes	No	Yes	Yes	Two pairs only.
131	Training gloves	Yes	Yes	No	Yes	Yes	To be kept in the gym. One pair only - lightweight.
132	Sponge	Yes	Yes	No	No	No	Ordinary domestic size.
133	Pony tail	Yes	Yes	No	Yes	Yes	One dozen maximum.
134	Belt	Yes	Yes	No	Yes	Yes	Only one. Maximum width 1", plain with attached buckle.
135	Computer hand/ portable	Yes	Yes	No	Yes	Yes	Only by application to the Governing Governor. No facility for connection to an external modem. For educational purposes only, not in cell unless with Governing Governor's approval.

INDEX

Compasses	64
Computers	135
Crockery	32
Cross/Crucifix and other religious items	83
Curtains	14
D	
Darts and Dart Flights	89
Diaries/Personal Organiser	109
E	
Earpiece for radio etc	6
Earring/Stud	33
F	
Flannel	101
Floor Mat	15
Flowers	34
Food Containers	35
Football Boots	90
Footwear (Indoors)	17
Footwear (Training Shoes/Basketball Boots)	18
Footwear (Weight Training Shoes)	19
G	
Games	29
Garden Seeds	65
Garment Shaver	113
Greeting Card	36
Gum Shield	91
H	
Hammer	75
Hairbrush	102

Typewriter	124
U	
Underpants	21
V	
Vacuum Flask	57
Varnish	80
W	
Watch	58
Weight Lifting Knee Supports	81
Weight Training Belt	126
Writing Pad and Envelopes	114
Wood	81
Wood or Leather Dye	82
X	
-	
Y	
-	
Z	
-	

Note

Inflammable Substances and Hazardous Adhesives.

The advice on the use of adhesives in prison which has been issued by DOC1 Division to all establishments should be used in conjunction with the following guidelines:-

1   No substance should be issued if it is known that there is a safer substitute or if it is not essential to the particular hobby for which it will be used.

2   Inflammable substances and hazardous adhesives should be held in and controlled from a suitable office or store and should only be issued to inmates between times specified by the Governor. They should only be issued in the quantity necessary for the work to be undertaken during that period and in amounts insufficient to create a significant hazard.

3   A record should be kept of each substance which goes out from and returns to the office or store.

Property list for one SSU inmate

Return of property to reception dated 6.10.94

Item(s)	Storage box number
Adaptor, 3 pin shaver	Box 9
Address book	Box 21
Address Book	Box 20
Aerial wire	Box 9
Aerosol fixture	Box 10
Aftershaves, assorted	Box 23
Analogue, Quartz	Box 22
Apron	Box 1
Back scrubber	Box 22
Bag, maroon cloth	Box 12
Bag, rag cloth	Box 12
Bags, plastic carrier, quantity	Box 9
Baking sheets	Box 1
Basket, fruit	Box 15
Bathrobe, green	Box 19
Batteries, Duracell x 4	Box 22
Beard trimmer	Box 23
Bed rug, blue	Box 18
Bedspread, blue and white	Box 8
Beer mat x 2	Box 20
Belt, brown leather	Box 19
Belt leather	Box 7
Belt, leather	Box 7
Belt, leather brown	Box 13

Biros assorted x 16	Box 22
Book, cartoon	Box 22
Bookmarks, leather x 6	Box 21
Books x 16	Box 21
Books x 2	Box 21
Boots, pair black zip up	Box 12
Boots, pair brown suede	Box 12
Boots, pair brown suede	Box 12
Bottle Clearasil	Box 22
Bottle Comfort	Box 13
Bottle Linseed oil	Box 11
Bottle nail hardener	Box 20
Bottle seal	Box 20
Bottle skin milk	Box 22
Bowl, pyrex	Box 2
Box, empty Aiwa cassette	Box 9
Box, empty beard trimmer	Box 9
Box, green cardboard	Box 13
Box of Xmas cards and envelopes	Box 22
Briefcase and assorted documents	Box 17
Brush, clothes	Box 20
Cake Board	Box 1
Cake Rack	Box 1
Calender 1994	Box 22
Calender 1994	Box 20
Cap	Box 7
Cap, furlined rain	Box 10
Cap, suede	Box 10
Cap, tartan	Box 10

Cardigan, blue	Box 10
Cardigan, dark blue	Box 19
Cardigan, red suede woollen	Box 13
Cards x 3	Box 20
Carrier bag	Box 22
Case, letter	Box 20
Casette player, SANYO	Box 22
Cassette tapes x 10	Box 21
Cassette tapes x 2	Box 21
Cassettes in case x 10	Box 21
Cassettes x 2	Box 22
Clock, travel	Box 20
Clothes cleaner	Box 22
Coathangers x 2	Box 13
Coffee cup and saucer	Box 22
Coffee cups and saucers x 4	Box 14
Coffee filter and pot x 2	Box 14
Coffee machine	Box 14
Coffee pot and filter	Box 17
Contact lens container	Box 20
Contact lens holder with lens	Box 22
Container plastic x 2	Box 22
Containers, quantity of plastic	Box 5
Cooking equipment, quantity of	Box 3
Cooking utensils	Box 6
Correspondence, papers	Box 5
Curtain	Box 20
Curtains, pair blue	Box 13
Deodorant x 3	Box 20

Diary 1993	Box 21
Diary, desk	Box 21
Dictionaries x 3	Box 20
Disc floppy	Box 17
Document case, plastic	Box 9
Double mirror (damaged)	Box 23
Drawing paper	Box 22
Egg cups, wooden x 2	Box 20
Envelopes, quantity	Box 20
Extension, 3 pin 2 point	Box 9
Face cream x 8	Box 22
First aid bag	Box 20
Flannels x 2	Box 19
Flipflops, pair	Box 22
Foodstuffs, quantity of	Box 6
Foodstuffs, quantity of	Box 1
Foodstuffs, quantity of	Box 2
Foodstuffs, quantity of	Box 4
Foodstuffs, quantity of	Box 17
Glass	Box 17
Glasses, crystal	Box 14
Gloves, packet disposable	Box 22
Gloves weight	Box 20
Hairbrush	Box 23
Handkerchief	Box 7
Handkerchief	Box 18
Handle wooden	Box 20
Hangers x 2	Box 16
Hat, blue woollen	Box 7

Hatstand	Box 15
Headphones	Box 20
Headphones	Box 9
Holdall, blue	Box 13
Holdalls x 3	Box 15
Hook, plastic	Box 9
Hooks, brass x 3	Box 9
Hooks, plastic x 2	Box 20
Insect repellant	Box 23
Jacket, green	Box 13
Jeans, blue demin	Box 19
Jeans, pair blue x 2	Box 13
Jeans, pair blue	Box 13
Joggers, pair black	Box 13
Jogging top, blue Puma	Box 8
Jogging trousers green	Box 19
Jumper, blue	Box 10
Jumper, blue	Box 19
Jumper, blue	Box 10
Jumper, blue crew neck	Box 7
Jumper, brown	Box 10
Jumper, grey	Box 10
Jumper, maroon	Box 10
Jumper, multi blue	Box 7
Jumper, purple Lacoste	Box 7
Jumper, red	Box 10
Jumper, white	Box 7
Key wallet	Box 17
Knife, Hobby x 2	Box 22

Knife palette	Box 22
Lace blue shoe	Box 9
Laces, brown pair	Box 7
Ladybird, woolly	Box 20
Lead	Box 20
Lead	Box 9
Lead, Audio	Box 9
Lead, extension (damaged)	Box 23
Letters, quantity	Box 20
Longjohns, beige	Box 7
Magazines, assorted	Box 13
Magazines, quantity	Box 22
Magazines, quantity	Box 14
Magazines, quantity	Box 21
Matches, book	Box 22
Mirror	Box 23
Mittens, pair leather	Box 13
Mug	Box 5
Mug, glass	Box 17
Mug, plastic	Box 4
Mug, pottery	Box 17
Nail scissors	Box 23
Oven glove	Box 1
Paintbrush, 25mm	Box 10
Paintbrush 50mm	Box 9
Paintbrushes assorted x 35	Box 11
Paintbrushes assorted x 35	Box 22
Painting, oil	Box 22
Painting, oil	Box 16

Painting, oil	Box 20
Pamphlets, quantity	Box 20
Pants, pair blue	Box 13
Papers, miscellaneous	Box 22
Paperwork, quantity	Box 20
Paperwork, quantity	Box 21
Pasta cutter	Box 1
Peeler, vegetable	Box 20
Pen tidy	Box 20
Pencil	Box 12
Pens, quantity	Box 20
Phonecard, 40 unit	Box 17
Photograph	Box 20
Photograph in frame	Box 20
Photograph in frame	Box 22
Photographs, quantity	Box 20
Photographs, quantity of	Box 17
Pillowcases, blue x 2	Box 18
Pillowcases, blue x 2	Box 7
Plates, dinner x 6	Box 14
Plates, side x 5	Box 14
Poster, Dutch x 2	Box 20
Poster, Mini Mouse	Box 20
Posy pouch	Box 17
Pouch, Roberts	Box 20
Radio, Roberts	Box 23
Radio, Roberts rambler	Box 9
Razor refills, packet	Box 22
Razors x 2	Box 23

Rosary and crucifix	Box 20
Sachets, 5mm sodium chlorate x 6	Box 22
Sachets, sodium chloride x 7	Box 22
Sanyo cassette recorder	Box 22
Saucepan	Box 1
Saucer	Box 17
Saucer	Box 2
Scarf, beige	Box 10
Scarf, blue	Box 7
Scissors	Box 20
Sellotape x 3 rolls	Box 9
Set square, plastic	Box 9
Shampoo, sachets Givenchy	Box 22
Shaver, brown	Box 23
Shaving brushes x 2	Box 23
Sheet, blue x 2	Box 7
Sheets, blue x 2	Box 18
Sheets, white x 2	Box 7
Shirt, beige casual	Box 7
Shirt, blue	Box 16
Shirt, blue FILA T/	Box 19
Shirt, blue Lacoste polo	Box 16
Shirt blue T/	Box 18
Shirt, blue T/	Box 13
Shirt, blue T/ x 2	Box 19
Shirt, brown check	Box 10
Shirt, cerise T/	Box 19
Shirt, check	Box 17
Shirt, green Frankshirter T/	Box 16

Shirt, green Lacoste T/	Box 16
Shirt, green polo	Box 16
Shirt, Leonards of London striped	Box 16
Shirt, light blue T/	Box 19
Shirt, Marlboro T/	Box 18
Shirt, misty green	Box 16
Shirt, multicheck	Box 10
Shirt, multicheck	Box 10
Shirt, multicoloured	Box 10
Shirt, red check	Box 10
Shirt, red polo	Box 16
Shirt, red T/	Box 19
Shirt, white Lacoste polo	Box 7
Shirt, white T/	Box 19
Shirt, white T/	Box 16
Shirt, white T/	Box 7
Shirt, white T/ x 2	Box 19
Shirt, white T/ x 2	Box 19
Shirt, white T/	Box 7
Shirt, white T/	Box 13
Shirt, white telethon T/	Box 18
Shirt, white tennis	Box 16
Shirt, yellow Lacoste polo	Box 16
Shirt, yellow T/	Box 7
Shirt, yellow T/	Box 17
Shirts, blue T/ x 6	Box 7
Shoebag, grey/white	Box 19
Shoes, pair	Box 12
Shoes, pair NIKE	Box 18

Shoes, pair NIKE	Box 17
Shoes, pair nylon running	Box 12
Shorts, blue jogger	Box 17
Shorts, pair blue x 2	Box 18
Shorts, pair grey jogging	Box 18
Shorts, pair NIKE black grey	Box 18
Shorts, white	Box 18
Skewer wooden kebab x 12	Box 20
Soap, bar	Box 22
Socks assorted x 5 pairs	Box 7
Socks, knitted	Box 18
Socks, pair green	Box 10
Socks, pair white x 2	Box 13
Socks, Pair green	Box 18
Socks, white x 3 pairs	Box 7
Speakers x 2 AIWA	Box 22
Spectacle case, metal	Box 22
Spectacle cases x 2	Box 20
Spectacle strap	Box 22
Spectacles	Box 20
Spectacles in case	Box 22
Spray	Box 23
Spray, mosquito	Box 23
Stamps, used, quantity	Box 22
Stamps x 2 2p	Box 22
Stamps x 5 25p	Box 22
Stamps x 58 5p	Box 22
Stapler	Box 20
Stickers, quantity of	Box 22

Sweat band	Box 20
Sweater, black	Box 10
Sweater, multicoloured	Box 7
Sweater, red	Box 10
Sweater, red polo neck	Box 7
Sweater, white polo neck	Box 19
Sweatshirt, blue	Box 8
Sweatshirt blue and white towelling	Box 7
Sweatshirt, green	Box 10
Sweatshirt, green and blue	Box 8
Sweatshirt maroon	Box 13
Sweatshirt, purple Home Counties	Box 7
Sweatshirts, grey x 2	Box 8
Tablets, vitamin x 100	Box 20
Tank top, Orange	Box 19
Tank top, Red	Box 19
Tea towel	Box 22
Teaspoon	Box 20
Telephone book	Box 20
Thermos flasks x 2	Box 17
Ties x 4	Box 7
Tin, biscuit	Box 9
Tin, biscuit containing misc items	Box 14
Tin of assorted pencils	Box 11
Toaster	Box 14
Toiletries contained in red container	Box 23
Toilette water, bottle Givenchy	Box 22
Toothbrush	Box 23
Toothbrush x 18	Box 22

Towel, Dior beach	Box 7
Towel, green	Box 7
Towel, green	Box 17
Towels, white with yellow stripe x 2	Box 7
Trackshirt bottoms, light green	Box 19
Trackshirt bottoms, pair blue	Box 17
Tracksuit, adidas	Box 19
Tracksuit, black Australian	Box 19
Tracksuit, blue	Box 19
Tracksuit bottoms, red	Box 7
Tracksuit, purple	Box 8
Tracksuit trousers, blue adidas	Box 19
Tracksuit trousers, Sergio Tacchini	Box 19
Trainers, pair Air-max	Box 12
Trainers, pair HI-TEC	Box 22
Trainers, pair LA Gear	Box 12
Trainers, pair NIKE	Box 12
Training shoes, pair NIKE	Box 12
Transformer	Box 22
Transformer and cable	Box 23
Trousers, brown cord	Box 10
Trousers, pair green	Box 13
Tub of skin cream	Box 23
Tub, plastic	Box 22
Tube of stain remover	Box 23
Tweezers	Box 23
Underpants pair grey x 2	Box 18
Underpants pair white x 2	Box 18
Underpants pair white striped	Box 18

Underpants pair white/blue x 4	Box 18
Underpants x 7	Box 7
Vest, Adidas	Box 18
Vest, grey	Box 19
Videos x 15	Box 21
Visor, golf	Box 22
Wallet	Box 17
Wash bag x 2	Box 23
Washing powder 'Bold' pkt	Box 16
Writing paper, quantity	Box 22
Writing paper, quantity	Box 20

Memorandum circulated on 9.8.94

From: [   ]

HMP WHITEMOOR

9 August 1994

To: [   ]

SSU

HMP WHITEMOOR

cc [   ]

RE: SSU PROCEDURES

I am extremely concerned about the lack of "ownership" of various areas of routine work within the SSU. I am au fait with the pressure of working within such a Unit, but there is a lot of slippage with basics and clearly both security and staff's safety are possibly at risk. Managers, if they want good ASRs, must demonstrate:

i.   that they are efficient and effective Managers.

ii.   that they are capable of improving and developing the area that they are accountable for.

Continually, when I ask someone to do quite a simple task it is not done properly or followed through to its logical conclusion. More often than not, it is referred back to me in one way or another and this is far from satisfactory! I do not wish to antagonise people, but work has to be completed at the appropriate rank and not repeatedly pushed upwards - let's have more of "look what I have solved", rather than the passing up of problems.

Areas that need attention are:

1.   Fridges/Freezers: A routine needs drawing up by an SO for any future loss. Staff must bag and remove all items claimed for. The items must be properly costed and identified, e.g. 1/4 full 40oz jar of Heinz ketchup original cost £1.60 - value 40p. Individual claims on Request/Complaint forms with one covering memo for the lot. [   ] (Finance) expects it right first time, so do I.

2.   Electric Leads in Cells: Not allowed. Whose leads are they? Why are they in the SSU? Danger to staff if they wire up doors etc. What are you doing about it?

3. Staff have served excessive periods of duty (3 years!) in the SSU - has anybody looked at this? Plenty of scope for changes within a group of Operations size. It is an easy job for Senior Officers and Principal Officers to liaise a change of staff, surely.

4. Letters going between the Segregation Unit and the SSU - only allowed having gone through both Correspondence Officers.

5. Security of the Visits area failing, probably during non-visiting times. £500 recently smuggled into the Unit and also 3 cameras. What else - a gun next? Should not all inmates be stripped each time they leave that sterile area without exception. THIS IS EXTREMELY SERIOUS, never mind the taking of photographs within the Unit compromising security and circumventing of the cash procedures. There is also a proper procedure for the use of cameras - why are we not adhering to it?

6. Phone Calls: These should be logged accurately, inmates should not have access to the logging sheets (some have gone missing!). The cost of the calls should be obtained from the computer printout from the switchboard and debited to the inmates' account weekly. Who is going to set this up professionally? It is basic Senior Officers work and should not need referring anywhere except amongst yourself.

7. Excessive property being allowed within the Unit - it is all over the place and is compromising security, health and safety, fire regulations, access etc. It is a collective problem that needs resolving - any ideas?

8. [   ]'s property - have we resolved how we are getting it to Ireland
    [   ]? We may be repatriating two more and this needs resolving
    properly.

I am sure that a lot of good work is being done within the SSU, but there should not be any expense spared. Slippage is awfully difficult to pull back and certainly should not be allowed to occur in a Special Security Unit within a maximum security prison. Can you all look at these areas and I shall be seeing you all individually over the next few days.

[   ]

Correspondence regarding privileges granted to SSU prisoners

Extract of letter dated 13 January 1994 from Member of Parliament to Home Secretary

"I visited the SSU unit for prisoners classified as likely to attempt to escape. They are housed in a separate building within the prison compound. The prisoners held are serving the same length of sentences as those in the ordinary 'A' and 'B' wings, that it is up to 25 years. I have to say that I am not surprised that no prisoner in the SSU unit wants to be transferred to the mainstream. It is far too comfortable. The wing has wall to wall carpeting, pictures on the wall, curtains, lampshades, soft furnishings, television and sitting room where Satellite TV is available, a dining room and very well equipped kitchen where they can prepare their own food the ingredients being brought in from outside, be it steak, smoked salmon etc (all these prisoners are wealthy).

There is also a computer room, a gymnasium, their own outdoor landscaped facilities, and up to two prison visits a day from friends and relations. Telephone calls can be made overseas albeit they have to pay for them and there is even a notice board listing the costs of calls to Australia, Italy and France etc.

The cells are better furnished with more personal input than the rest of the prison and the bathroom facilities are good.

Bearing in mind that these men are not serving any longer sentences in prison than those in categories A and B, I wonder why we have to spend a disproportionate amount of money giving them such hotel-style conditions."

Extract of briefing note from Director General to Home Secretary dated 11 March 1994

"You asked for advice about the letter of 13 January from [   ] MP about Whitemoor ...

Facilities for prisoners in the Special Secure Unit

The Special Secure Unit is for exceptionally high risk category A prisoners. It is not a segregation unit for those who have misbehaved in prison. Some prisoners live in the SSU for many years. They have no access to staff or prisoners outside the unit, workshops, education and training facilities, the library or the prison shop. In these circumstances, the regime is limited to catering, gardening, hobbies and PE. From my own inspection, I know it is extremely claustrophobic. The decision to make the surroundings marginally more comfortable was taken when the prison was built, in order to provide a modest counterbalance to some of the more draconian aspects of the environment and regime. Prisoners are allowed to make telephone calls for up to an hour each month. For those in the SSU who are foreign nationals, and who receive no visit from their family, the telephone call is their only method of direct communication with their families. There is no security risk, as the calls are monitored and taped."

Extract of reply to Member of Parliament from Home Secretary dated 21 March 1994

"The Special Secure Unit is for prisoners who have both sufficient resources to escape, and who would present a considerable danger to the community if they succeeded. Many prisoners serve many years in the Unit which is a very confined space which they will only leave if they are ill and need hospital treatment. For this reason, I understand that prisoners in the Unit experience a much more limited regime in comparison to other prisoners in Whitemoor and have no access to workshops, education and training facilities or outside PE facilities. The surroundings which you saw were designed to compensate to some extent for the regime inside the Unit. Prisoners in the Special Secure Unit are allowed to make telephone calls at public expense only to people on an approved list. Some of the prisoners are foreign nationals who receive no visitors, and whose only direct contact with their families is through a telephone call. These calls are limited to one hour a month and are taped and monitored by security staff."

Incidents Recorded at HMP Whitemoor 30th April 1994 to 9th September 1994

DATE	INCIDENT SUMMARY
30/04/94	Assault on Officer by inmate.
30/04/94	Assault on Officer by inmate.
30/04/94	Assault on a Senior Officer by inmate.
30/04/94	Assault on Officer by inmate.
02/05/94	Cell fire
02/05/94	Inmate attempted suicide
02/05/94	Small fire outside 'C' Wing Red Spur.
12/05/94	Small fire S/Unit - confined to window of cell cage.
19/05/94	Officer assaulted by inmate.
21/05/94	Small fire 'B' Wing shower, Blue Spur
21/05/94	Attempted hostage taking by inmate.
28/05/94	Assault, inmate on inmate.
31/05/94	Death of inmate - natural cause.
05/06/94	Inmate threats to cut throat.
05/06/94	Inmate threatened to cut wrists. False claim.
11/06/94	Inmate in possession of cannabis resin.
12/06/94	Inmate assaulted another inmate.
12/06/94	Concerted indiscipline of five inmates on 'C' Wing exercise - refused to leave yard. Inmates removed by C & R Teams.
14/06/94	Inmate in possession of cannabis resin.
24/06/94	Officer assaulted by inmate.
24/06/94	Inmate in possession of an opiate.
24/06/94	Officer assaulted by inmate.

27/06/94	Inmate admitted to Peterborough District Hospital.
27/06/94	Assault on Officer by inmate in 'B' wing.
28/06/94	Senior Officer and Customs Officer assaulted by inmate.
30/06/94	Assault (with excrement) by inmate on Officer.
01/07/94	Fight between two inmates.
01/07/94	Assault by inmate on Officer.
03/07/94	Assault on fellow inmate 'C' wing.
04/07/94	Inmate smashes up his cell.
05/07/94	Fire in cell occupied by inmate.
07/07/94	Alleged assault on inmate by persons unknown.
12/07/94	Lock down search of 'C' & 'D' re loss of knife.
14/07/94	Inmate sets fire to rubbish in cell.
19/07/94	Loss of knife on 'D' Wing.
20/07/94	Governor assaulted by inmate.
21/07/94	Three inmates barricaded cell in 'C' Wing.
25/07/94	Inmate assaults another inmate.
27/07/94	Inmate assaults another inmate.
28/07/94	Cell fire Seg. Unit, while occupied by inmate.
01/08/94	Assault on inmate by persons unknown.
02/08/94	Cell fire ('D' Wing), occupied by an inmate.
02/08/94	Fight between inmates - injuries to both inmates - knife involved.
02/08/94	Inmate set fire to rubbish in cell.
04/08/94	Nurse assaulted by inmate.
08/08/94	Inmate slammed door on officer's hand.
09/08/94	Death of inmate in Brighton Hospice 09/08/94 (Natural Causes).

13/08/94	Assault on Officer by inmate.
13/08/94	Assault on Senior Officer by inmate.
22/08/94	Petition against smoking.
23/08/94	Assault by inmate on Officer.
24/08/94	Closure of Workshop 1 and refusal to work.
25/08/94	Twelve prisoners adjudicated on. Normal work resumed.
26/08/94	Key compromise 26/08/94 on 'D' Wing - full lock change of prison.
27/08/94	Officer bitten by inmate on 'D' Wing.
27/08/94	Assault on Officer by inmate on 'D' Wing, Blue Spur.
30/08/94	Assault on inmate by unknown assailants.
03/09/94	Assault on inmate by fellow inmate - 'C' Wing.
02/09/94	Inmate found in possession of cannabis.
04/09/94	Inmate assaulted by another inmate.
04/09/94	Inmate found in possession of a controlled drug - Cannabis. Proved positive.
06/09/94	Assault by one inmate on another.
07/09/94	Attempted suicide by inmate.
09/09/94	Escape from SSU.

HMSO Publications are available from:

HMSO Publications Centre
(Mail, fax and telephone orders only)
PO Box 276, London SW8 5DT
Telephone orders 0171-873 9090
General enquiries 0171-873 0011
(queuing system in operation for both numbers)
Fax orders 0171-873 8200

HMSO Bookshops
49 High Holborn, London WC1V 6HB
(counter service only)
0171-873 0011 Fax 0171-831 1326
68-69 Bull Street, Birmingham B4 6AD
0121-236 9696 Fax 0121-236 9699
33 Wine Street, Bristol BS1 2BQ
0117 926 4306 Fax 0117 929 4515
9-21 Princess Street, Manchester M60 8AS
0161-834 7201 Fax 0161-833 0634
16 Arthur Street, Belfast BT1 4GD
01232 238451 Fax 01232 235401
71 Lothian Road, Edinburgh EH3 9AZ
0131-228 4181 Fax 0131-229 2734

HMSO's Accredited Agents
(see Yellow Pages)

and through good booksellers

ISBN 0-10-127412-2

9 780101 274128

for GCSE
COMPUTER STUDIES

Confidence is the key to success.

When it comes to exam preparation for GCSE exams or for Scottish Standard Grade, students know they can trust Letts to get it right. Letts Study Guides offer year-round course backup, convenient reference AND an approach to revision that really works. Clear and concise, the new-look Letts will help you prepare sensibly – confidently – for exam success.

This Computer Studies Study Guide contains:

◄ For each board, detailed analysis of the syllabus and exam structure.

◄ Explanatory text – to help you allocate the right amount of time and effort to your study and revision.

◄ Guided question practice, to test your knowledge and sharpen your exam technique.

◄ Practical help with the techniques and tricks of study and coursework, revision and exams.

Letts authors are up-to-date subject specialists, as well as experienced teachers and examiners.

Whatever the question, the answer is Letts.

GCSE / KEY STAGE 4 STUDY GUIDES

Biology (KS4)	History	German
Business Studies	Human Biology	Geography
Chemistry (KS4)	Mathematics (KS4)	French
Computer Studies	Physics (KS4)	English (KS4)
Economics	Science (KS4)	Sociology
	Sociology	Technology (KS4)
	World History	

ISBN 1-85758-303-5

Syllabus coverage

GCSE

MEG
NEAB
NICCEA
SEG
ULEAC
WJEC

STANDARD GRADE

SEB

123 p. 157 yllaitini